Creating Sensory Smart Classrooms

Creating Sensory Smart Classrooms introduces educators to the foundations of sensory processing and offers tools to meet the wide variety of sensory needs in each classroom. This comprehensive handbook helps readers understand the neurobiology behind sensory processing and regulation issues, recognize when a student is over- or under-stimulated, and integrate different sensory inputs into the school environment. Practical and accessible chapters foster an understanding of how sensory processing influences behaviors in the classroom and how protective relationships, combined with sensory strategies, positively influence students' regulation for improved learning outcomes. Packed with useful examples, this is essential reading for teachers looking to develop the knowledge and skills they need to design sensory smart environments that support ALL learners.

Jamie Chaves is a pediatric occupational therapist with over nine years of experience working with children who have sensory processing differences and learning differences.

Ashley Taylor is a clinical pediatric psychologist with over 15 years of experience working with young children and their families, specializing in conducting comprehensive psychological, psychoeducational, and developmental evaluations.

Creating Sensory Smart Classrooms

A Practical Guide for Educators

Jamie Chaves and Ashley Taylor

Routledge
Taylor & Francis Group

NEW YORK AND LONDON

First published 2021
by Routledge
52 Vanderbilt Avenue, New York, NY 10017

and by Routledge
2 Park Square, Milton Park, Abingdon, Oxon OX14 4RN

Routledge is an imprint of the Taylor & Francis Group, an informa business

© 2021 Jamie Chaves and Ashley Taylor

Library of Congress Cataloging-in-Publication Data
A catalog record for this title has been requested

ISBN: 978-0-367-50686-5 (hbk)
ISBN: 978-0-367-50101-3 (pbk)
ISBN: 978-1-003-05079-7 (ebk)

Typeset in Optima
by Newgen Publishing UK

Contents

Meet the Authors

Jamie Chaves, OTD, OTR/L, SWC, is a pediatric occupational therapist with over 9 years of experience working with children who have sensory processing differences and learning differences. She received bachelor degrees in Health Science and Psychology from Bradley University, and a doctorate of Occupational Therapy from Washington University School of Medicine in St. Louis. Dr. Chaves is the division leader for the occupational therapy department at The Center for Connection in Pasadena, CA—a multidisciplinary clinic that provides an array of services rooted in the IPNB framework. She recognizes the importance of a play-based, relationship-based approach to therapy that is rooted in regulation. She does contract work with various private schools in Pasadena, CA, particularly delivering teacher in-services and parent education on a variety of topics including promoting positive handwriting, sensory integration strategies in the classroom, how diet and sleep influence learning and regulation, and the impact of screen time on development and learning. Dr. Chaves lives in Pasadena, CA with her husband and two young children. This is Dr. Chaves' second book with Dr. Ashley Taylor.

Ashley Taylor, Psy.D., is a licensed clinical pediatric psychologist with a practice in Pasadena, CA. She is endorsed in California as an infant-family and early childhood mental health specialist. Dr. Taylor received bachelor's degrees in psychology and Spanish from the University of Vermont in Burlington, VT, and attended the Wright Institute in Berkeley, CA, for her graduate training. She has worked in Vermont, Massachusetts, and California supporting children, families, and educators for over 15 years. She specializes in providing comprehensive pediatric evaluations assessing for developmental delays, autism, trauma, ADHD, and learning disabilities. She also provides parent–child dyadic mental health therapy as well as educator and parent trainings and workshops. She has provided evaluations and mental health services for the pediatric population across multiple settings including intensive day treatment programs, medical settings, schools, community mental health, and private practice. She believes in the power of building healthy relationships to build healthy brains! Dr. Taylor is also the mom to two fun and active boys who are always ready for the next big adventure!

Preface

Something Jamie tells parents all the time is that we can only act on the knowledge that we have at any given point. We all have different capacities for taking in knowledge, similar to how we all process sensory information differently. If we take in too much at once we may become flooded or overwhelmed. This may cause us to shut down, run away from, or avoid the information presented. This book is meant to complement the amazing work you are already doing to shape the lives and minds of our children. If at any point you feel flooded, take a step back. Use the knowledge you have at that point to move forward. Teachers, you are already asked to do so much. This book is a way to further equip you to better understand what might be causing certain behaviors you see in your students, not a means to overwhelm you.

Our decision to write this book stems from the curiosity of dozens of teachers we've worked with over the years who have made observations and asked questions about sensory processing differences amongst their students. The structure and content contained in these pages was essentially born out of a sensory processing seminar that Jamie has conducted on multiple occasions with educators and therapists seeking to learn more about the topic to better understand the needs of their students and clients. The teachers have noticed an upward trend in the sensory needs of students, yet they feel under-equipped to help support these needs. It's true that less outdoor play time, more screen time, more structured activities, and longer school days have likely impacted the sensory needs of students within the school environment. The information in this book is a starting point for educators to understand the effects of sensory processing on learning, structure the school environment to support a wide variety of sensory needs, and connect students with the appropriate resources to maximize their learning potential.

Sensory processing, and its corresponding influence on regulation, behavior, and learning, is a complex subject. There is still much to be learned through research. All of the concepts in this book are highly interconnected and difficult to tease apart. The information in these chapters is not meant to train you to be an occupational therapist, neurologist, or psychologist. Rather, it is meant to give you a different lens through which you can look at a student's behavior and reflect on how sensory processing may be impacting their ability to participate in school-based activities. It is also meant to give you a lens through which you can look at your own sensory preferences and sensory environment in the classroom in order to influence your own regulation and the engagement of your students. Each teacher and student brings his or her unique sensory and motor needs to the classroom each day. In this book, we will explore what those sensory needs might be for us as adults, as well as for the students that we work with. Not only will this information help you as a teacher to better take care of yourself, navigate stressful situations, and build regulation, it will also allow you to develop a foundation of knowledge regarding sensorimotor integration that you can adapt to your classroom and use to help connect with your students and support them in reaching their potential.

One of the authors, Jamie, has dedicated her career to working with children with sensory processing disorders. This book represents a compilation of resources she has read, continuing education and mentorship she has received, and nearly a decade of clinical experience. The other author, Ashley, began learning about sensory processing and sensorimotor integration when she was first introduced to the world of infant and early childhood mental health. They both have learned an incredible amount by looking at the world through the lens of sensory processing and sensorimotor integration, and how they influence relationships, regulation, and behavior. This knowledge is important for us as adults to learn about our own sensory preferences and aversions, and especially for those of us who work with children. As adults, we spend so much of our time talking, problem solving, multi-tasking and doing, we forget to slow down, pay attention to the present moment, and just be. There is no better way to do this than to develop an awareness of our senses and to tune into our bodies. Not only can sensory information guide and support our own awareness and regulation, but it can also profoundly impact our understanding of the behaviors of the children that we work with. As parents, both Jamie and Ashley have noticed how two children from the same family can have such incredibly different sensory preferences and sensory needs-- and the same is true for the children with whom they work.

Jamie and Ashley had the opportunity to collaborate together previously when they wrote the book *The "Why" Behind Classroom Behaviors: Integrative Strategies for Learning, Regulation, and Relationships.* In that book they detailed the concepts of brain organization, co-regulation, the teacher–student dyad, and learning differences, all of which complement the information in this book. They also preliminarily explored how sensory integration and regulation were connected, and how they impact both teachers and students within the classroom environment. This book is meant to expound on the concepts of sensory processing and sensory integration in order to provide you with even more knowledge and strategies to utilize in your classroom. Some of the information and diagrams from that book have been reused here with permission.

Acknowledgments

We are grateful for those of you who helped to shape this book. First and foremost, to parents and teachers with whom we have collaborated over the years: we have learned an incredible amount from you and your students. As a general note, all the names and identifying details in the vignettes and scenarios have been edited to protect the privacy of individuals and families.

To Kristy Lawson, OTD, OTR/L, SWC, CHES and Jennifer Olsen: thank you for taking the time to read the manuscript drafts and provide invaluable feedback.

To the researchers doing the important work that shapes and directs the clinical work we do on a daily basis, we commend you. To the occupational therapists driving the knowledge base and best practices related to sensory integration: Star Institute and Lucy Jane Miller, PhD, OTR, Erna Blanche, PhD, OTR/L, FAOTA, Winnie Dunn, OTR, FAOTA, Sharon Cermak, EdD, OTR/L, FAOTA, and Jeanetta Burpee, M.Ed, OTR/L, to name a few. To the neuroscientists who shape our understanding of the brain, relationships, and regulation: Stephen Porges, PhD, Dan Siegel, MD, Norman Doidge, MD, Bruce Perry, MD, PhD, and Ross Greene, PhD. To our mentors and contemporaries from whom we've learned so much: Tina Payne Bryson, PhD, Janel Umfress, CCC-SLP, Mona Delahooke, PhD, Barbara Shroud, PhD, Freddie Berger, OTR/L, and Daniel Franklin, PhD.

Ashley is thankful for her two sons, Jackson and Henry, who teach her new things every day, and especially how to enjoy the sensory world around us. Jamie sends her love to Kaylin and Mateo who, despite their vastly different sensory profiles, both find incredible joy exploring, being curious, and connecting with others. We both appreciate that being moms has made us better clinicians.

A huge special thank you to Hunt Dougherty for creating all of the images for this book. We're grateful for your time and creative genius.

Jamie acknowledges that writing a book with two children under the age of 3 during a pandemic is certainly not an ideal circumstance. Without the support of her husband, Francisco, this would not be possible. Glory to Christ who leads with love; "taste and see that the Lord is good."

Finally, we are grateful that Routledge took a chance on two clinicians aspiring to become authors. Thank you for your guidance and understanding throughout this process. We know this information will benefit so many educators, parents, and clinicians.

Setting the Stage for Learning with Sensory Processing

Humans are naturally curious and inquisitive—you will see that if you spend even five minutes with a toddler—which facilitates the intrinsic motivation for learning. Sensory information is one of the drivers of this desire to explore, discover, and do. Input from our senses influences how we relate to the environment, how we relate to ourselves, and how we relate to others. It gives meaning to activities and experiences. We cannot engage in the learning process without our senses—they serve as necessary building blocks. Sensory processing impacts every area of learning, attention, and regulation although it is often overlooked or not fully understood. The way in which we take in and utilize sensory input influences how we move our bodies, learn new skills, attend, and participate in everyday activities.

While we all have different ways of learning and doing through the use of sensory input, there are some basic organizational features of the brain that exist in every human. This organization is important in understanding the influence of sensory input on regulation and learning. We will quickly discuss a few brain-based constructs here to provide some background to better understand the concepts throughout the book.

Organization of the Brain and Neuroplasticity

One way that we can look at the organization of the brain is from the bottom of the brain to the top, or from the brainstem up to the cerebral cortex. This is called vertical organization. Lower levels of the brain are responsible for more primitive functions (i.e., breathing, blinking, heart rate, strong emotions) and are more readily accessed than the higher levels of the brain, which are responsible for conscious control and complex thinking (i.e., learning, problem solving, decision making, regulation).[1,2] More specifically, from the bottom of the brain to the top:

- The brainstem controls involuntary functions such as heart rate, breathing, blood pressure, and motor reflexes
- The midbrain is responsible for sensory and motor processing necessary for understanding the body and environment
- The limbic system houses the emotional regulation centers that allow for a calm, alert state of functioning
- The cerebral cortex is where higher-level thinking, problem solving, engagement, and organization skills occur

This organization plays a critical role in a student's ability to fully participate in the learning process. If, for example, a student is not able to appropriately process certain sensory information then that area of the brain becomes more responsive, making it more difficult for the student to attain emotional regulation and engage in the problem solving necessary to complete a given task such as a math worksheet. The higher levels of the brain, such as the prefrontal cortex, cannot adequately do their job unless the "needs" of the lower brain have been met.[1] In other words, the lower levels of the brain need to experience a sense of calm, safety, regulation, and the ability to process sensorimotor input appropriately in order for students to access the upper parts of their brain that allow them to focus, listen, think critically, and engage in the learning process. Ultimately, the integration of all the vertical layers becomes an essential foundation for learning.

Another important concept of learning is **neuroplasticity**—the brain's ability to change based on experiences.[3] Sensory experiences highly influence the connections made in the brain starting at birth. Relationships, development, emotional responses, and behavior are other examples of constructs that influence neuroplasticity. As you will continue to see throughout this book, sensory input is one very important way in which neuroplasticity of the brain occurs. It is important to realize that neuroplasticity can work in your favor or work against you. A commonly used phrase is, "if you don't use it, you'll lose it." Essentially, this means that the more you do something, learn something, or experience something

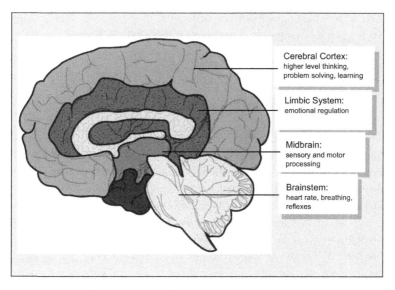

Figure 1.1 Vertical Organization of the Brain

One way the brain is organized is vertically, from the brainstem to the cerebral cortex—or the bottom to the top. The needs of the lower, more primitive areas of the brain must be established before the higher, more complex areas of the brain can do their job. This demonstrates that sensory processing and regulation are foundations for the academic and social demands at school.

Adapted from Perry, B. D. (1999). *Memories of Fear: How the Brain Stores and Retrieves Physiological States, Feeling, Behaviors and Thoughts from Traumatic Events. Splintered reflections: Images of the Body in Trauma.* New York: Basic Books.

emotionally, the more solid those connections in your brain will become. Because of something called "pruning" the connections in the brain that we do not use get reduced or eliminated over time.[4] Just like learning anything new, such as learning how to tie our shoes, ride a bike, drive a car, or learn a new language, it is hard at first because we don't have the neural connections in our brain to know how to do it. However, with repeated practice, it becomes easier as the pathways or connections in our brain become solidified and automatic. Because of neuroplasticity we can actually change our brain![3] We have to be mindful, however, of the actions we take, because the repeated behaviors that we engage in make those connections in our brain more solid, and eventually harder to change. For example, if a student learns to use a fisted grasp on a pencil in the first three years of handwriting without any correction, it will become increasingly challenging to change his grasp because those neural connections have become strengthened over the years.

Defining Regulation

While the focus of this book is on sensory processing, the concept of regulation is closely intertwined. A firm understanding of regulation will help to provide context and a foundation to the importance of applying knowledge of sensorimotor integration into the classroom environment. Regulation is a term that you've heard before because of its widespread use, but it can have different meanings depending on the context. Thus, it is important that we delineate what we mean when we use the word regulation throughout this book and how we apply it to our work with teachers and students. **Regulation** *is a broad term that describes an "individual's ability to manage his or her internal emotional and physical state in order to stay calm and engaged."*[1] This requires adequate behavioral organization—the ability to achieve an optimal arousal level in order to effectively handle the demands placed on oneself. Regulation often goes hand in hand with our arousal level. When regulation occurs in students, they can access the upper parts of their brain which allows them to communicate, solve problems, learn, connect with others, sit and focus, follow directions, complete school assignments, and make decisions.[1] In order for teaching and learning to occur, there must first be a foundation of regulation.

Physiologically, regulation occurs when there is, essentially, a balance between the sympathetic and parasympathetic branches of the nervous system.[1]

- The *sympathetic nervous system* helps "activate and arouse us into a state of action."[1] Additionally, it helps us attend to novel and relevant sensory information. When the sympathetic nervous system is *too* engaged a "fight or flight" response is triggered, likely resulting in one becoming overaroused, anxious, hyperactive, or angry.[1]

- The *parasympathetic nervous system* helps "slow us down and prepares us for rest."[1] This system also helps us to habituate (or "get used to") sensory information so we don't get too overwhelmed. If something is perceived as threatening, the parasympathetic nervous system can also be triggered. When the parasympathetic nervous system is *too* engaged, a "freeze" response is triggered, likely resulting in one becoming underaroused, depressed, sluggish, or passive.[1]

For many, the brain and body maintain this balance unconsciously to carry out daily activities. This allows us to divert more energy and resources to higher levels of the brain. There are instances throughout the day, however, where we use conscious control to regain a balance in these systems: taking a deep breath when we become frustrated or getting up to walk around when we feel lethargic, for example.

A balance between the sympathetic and parasympathetic nervous systems allows students to remain in a calm, alert state that sets the stage for learning. It allows them to feel safe and connected in order to explore and engage with others. When the sympathetic nervous system is activated because a student feels anxious about an upcoming test, the parasympathetic nervous system kicks in to ease that anxiety and bring the nervous system back into equilibrium.[1] This can be done through strategies like taking a deep breath or fidgeting with a pen, or it can be done through co-regulating with a friend or teacher. Until a balance is achieved the student will tend to demonstrate behaviors that are either more rigid (being inflexible or controlling)

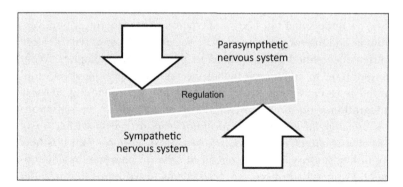

Figure 1.2 Regulation as a Balancing Act

Regulation—one's ability to manage his or her internal emotional and physical state in order to stay calm and engaged—occurs when the parasympathetic ("rest and digest") and sympathetic ("fight or flight") nervous systems are in balance. When these systems are in balance we achieve a calm, alert state that is required for attentive cognitive engagement.

or chaotic (feeling "out of control" or unstable).[5] These behaviors are a way of communicating dysregulation—an imbalance between the sympathetic and parasympathetic nervous systems. *This is critically important to recognize in the classroom: when a student is dysregulated they are less able to access the higher levels of their brain, which results in a decreased capacity to pay attention, learn, and integrate new information.* With the high demands that exist in a school environment—from the academic workload to social engagement to sensory stimulation—achieving a state of regulation is even more important in order to optimize learning.[1]

Foundations of Sensory Processing in the Classroom

One of the ways in which the sympathetic and parasympathetic nervous systems achieve and maintain balance is through processing of sensory information within the environment and within the body. **Sensory processing** *is defined as "the ability to receive, manage, and interpret messages from each sensory system."*[1] Basically, it is how we respond to sensory input. While traditionally we think of the five external sensory systems (sight, sound, touch, taste, smell), there are actually three additional internal sensory systems that influence how we understand our body and environment (proprioception, vestibular, and interoception). All of these sensory systems will be more intricately defined and explored in the upcoming chapters. What is important to know here is that the appropriate integration of all of the sensory systems is a critical foundation for learning. **Sensory integration** *is our brain's "ability to orchestrate all of the sensations into meaningful behavioral and motor responses without becoming too overwhelmed, distracted, or disengaged."*[1] Simply put, it is how we utilize sensory input in concert in order to navigate the environment. We need all of our sensory systems to work together in order for us to be able to move through our day in a regulated way and perform the tasks required of us. Thus, the sum of all our sensory systems is greater than the individual parts.

Let's take a minute to look at one way in which sensory processing occurs. When a sensory input is presented to the brain from the environment, the brain is activated in a certain manner to determine if the input

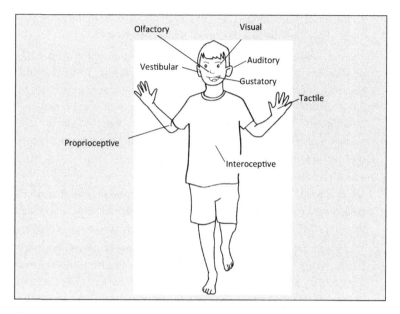

Figure 1.3 Sensory Systems

This diagram illustrates the location of the sensory receptors for each of the sensory systems. Visual, auditory, tactile, gustatory (taste), and olfactory (smell) input is all external while vestibular, proprioceptive, and interoceptive input is all internal.

Taken from Chaves, J. & Taylor, A. (2020). *The "Why" Behind Classroom Behaviors: Integrative Strategies for Learning, Regulation, and Relationships*. Thousand Oaks, CA: Corwin.

is important. Does this information require more attention, or is it unimportant and can it be ignored (at least unconsciously)? Quite a few areas of the brain and nervous system are activated when presented with certain sensory information in order to determine whether and in which way we need to react or respond to each situation.

- First the sensory input has to be noticed and attended to. This is done when the sympathetic nervous system alerts the prefrontal cortex, the complex-thinking and decision-making part of the brain.

  If we hear a dog barking loudly while sitting at a café, we will likely perk up or even turn toward the noise (auditory input).

- As the input is attended to, an emotional response from the amygdala occurs based on the level of threat that is perceived.

  You may feel a flood of fear if you detect a threat from the dog's bark, or you may feel ambivalent if you detect no threat. This emotional response is often impacted by your previous experiences with dogs. Do dogs bring up memories of safety and fun, or of being bitten and traumatized? Your previous experiences with dogs will impact the response of your nervous system and ultimately your emotional reaction to the sensory input of the dog barking.

- The hypothalamus is then activated in order to take immediate action to respond to the situation. If the nervous system perceives the situation to be a threat to your safety then a fight, flight, or freeze response will occur; the sympathetic or parasympathetic nervous system will be fully engaged.

  Your heart rate may increase due to the release of adrenaline, your palms may get sweaty, and you may feel tense because you sense that the dog may lunge toward you. You may even move to a different table at the café if you've had negative past experiences related to dogs. This threat response will impact your ability to enjoy your meal, talk with your friends, or attend to reading a book. This is because your nervous system has told you that you are in danger and it is doing everything it can to make sure you stay safe.

- If, on the other hand, the input is determined to be non-threatening or unimportant, the parasympathetic nervous system will help to calm the body back down and allow it to carry on with the previous task.

  When you further assess the situation, you notice the dog is on a leash, the dog is smaller than you first anticipated, and the dog is barking at a squirrel up a tree (not at you). You notice your heart rate start to slow and you can relax knowing that you will be safe. You can then easily return your attention to your café experience.

- When a similar sensory input is experienced in the future, the hippocampus plays a role in helping the brain to habituate (or get used to) to the sensory input. This way a threat response will not be experienced each time that input is encountered.

  Several minutes later when the dog barks again at the café, you don't even need to stop and look (or may not even hear the dog bark) because you know that you are safe.

So you can see, now, how sensory input can impact our sense of safety and regulation, as well as our state of attention and engagement with the world around us. If something as simple as a dark barking can send certain students into a heightened state of nervous system arousal, it can also impact their ability to focus, learn, and listen in the classroom setting. Now think about how many different sensory inputs there are in your classroom, and how they might impact the state of regulation for you and your students.

You may be wondering: how are we not constantly overwhelmed with sensory information all the time? This is because, as mentioned, when the brain starts to habituate to responses, we do not attend to them as readily. For example, our saliva actually has a taste to it, but if we constantly were stimulated by the taste of our saliva it would be incredibly overstimulating—this would make it more difficult to attend to other more salient sensory inputs. Consequently, the brain does not respond as readily to certain sensory inputs that are not deemed important in order to free up neural resources for other activities.

After repeated exposure and experiences, the brain, primarily the amygdala, basically files away emotional memories for the sensory inputs to draw on when similar situations arise in the future. These memory files may be positive, negative, or neutral. The more positive sensory experiences we have during the early years of life helps set the stage for curious engagement in the environment and regulated learning.[6] Playing at the beach in the sand, the smell of chocolate chip cookies, hearing *Twinkle Twinkle Little Star*, going down the slide at the playground—all of these may elicit positive emotional memories because they were positive sensory experiences as a child. In contrast, the more negative experiences we have early on, the more the brain gets wired to be in a reactive state which can result in hesitancy to explore and interact with the environment thus impeding the learning process. Wearing an itchy sweater, the smell of a rotten egg, hearing booming fireworks, spinning too fast on a merry-go-round—all of these may elicit negative emotional memories because they were negative sensory experiences as a child. (It's worth mentioning that genetics also play a role in how children respond to sensory information and process emotional experiences.)

Stress can also influence the perception of sensory experiences because the release of stress hormones, cortisol and adrenaline, actually prevent the prefrontal cortex (the complex-thinking and decision-making part of the brain) from shifting attention away from the sensory input, thus preserving the heightened state of arousal.[1] This causes us to focus more on the seemingly noxious sensory input rather than other things happening in the environment or other tasks at-hand. For example, during a recent trip to an aquarium, one of the authors, Jamie, touched a sea cucumber for the first time. She had a vague idea of what this creature might feel like, but she could still feel her anxiety increase as her hand approached it—her sympathetic nervous system was being activated. While touching the sea cucumber she heard voices in the background but was not processing at all what they were saying. Apparently her husband was asking her a question about where they wanted to go next. Her prefrontal cortex had shifted her focus completely to the sea cucumber experience to the point where she was unable to engage socially. But after touching the sea cucumber her parasympathetic nervous system was activated to get her back to a regulated state—her brain processed that she was safe despite experiencing something new. After several times of feeling the slimy texture and knowing what to anticipate, her sympathetic nervous system was less activated. She was able to engage in a conversation *while* touching the creature. In a similar way, if students are feeling stressed about certain sensory inputs in the environment—whether overtly or covertly—they may have difficulty shifting their attention away from those inputs in order to focus on the academic work in the classroom, social engagement at recess, or packing up at the end of the day.

Our behavioral responses, therefore, are a direct result of how well we take in, process, and integrate the sensory input being received.[6] At first glance it would seem that Jamie was just simply ignoring her husband, based on her behavior. However, she was literally not processing what he was saying to her because her brain was in a heightened state of regulation due to the stress of the new sensory experience. This happens all the time in the classroom as well. A student may be bothered so much by the tag in their shirt that they miss the instructions to take out their homework. A student may be so distracted by the smell of the banana in the trash can that they can't focus to complete their math worksheet. A student may feel so emotionally flooded from the sound of the pencil sharpener that they start to sing aloud. As teachers it is important not to jump to conclusions about a student's behavior. By maintaining a curious and open outlook, you can dive deeper to investigate a student's behavior. This may lead you to find that the student is not intentionally misbehaving or being disruptive, but they are in fact not taking in or processing sensory input in an appropriate way. As a result, their ability to regulate, focus, and learn will be compromised.

In infancy and childhood, a well-rounded variety of sensory experiences is important for the brain to grow and increase the connections made between different brain regions because sensory experiences inform the way we move, discover our bodies, and experience the world.[7,9] These experiences also help the brain habituate to sensory input that is safe and familiar, allowing the brain to focus on other things in the environment. This is why providing rich sensory experiences early on in life helps to facilitate development and learning. Variety also helps strengthen the associations the brain makes and add meaning to those associations, which is an important foundation for learning. For example, standing on one foot inside on the carpet, inside on a pillow, outside on the grass, and outside on woodchips all provide unique sensory opportunities that further strengthen the skill of balancing. Alternatively, exploring with our hands in shaving cream, sand, Play-doh, and water all give different tactile sensations to increase our body awareness. *When we are in a safe, regulated state*, the brain craves novelty and stimulation—lack thereof causes boredom and a longing for something different. In classrooms it is important to "change things up", offering a wide range of sensory-based learning experiences to strengthen brain integration. The end of this chapter discusses practical ways in which you can do this.

As a note, which we explore further in Chapter 3, there may be students in your classroom who have certain sensory processing differences that send their nervous system into a threat response when presented with new or different sensory input. Changing activities in the classroom may be overwhelming because that interferes with predictability and routine. Even though a variety of sensory-based learning experiences is important for these students, the way in which they receive these experiences will differ from other students. They may need additional support and intervention with an occupational therapist; additionally, throughout this book we will outline ways to scaffold sensory experiences in the classroom so that they can begin to process and experience certain sensory inputs in a safe way.

Classifying Sensory Processing

Researchers and clinicians continue to learn more and more about the way in which we process sensory information. Right now, we know that sensory processing can be broken down into three distinct categories depending on how the information is being used: sensory modulation, sensory

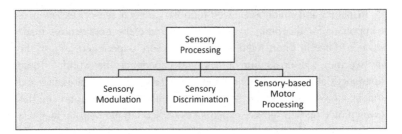

Figure 1.4 Classification of Sensory Processing

The way in which we process sensory information is grouped into three distinct categories. *Sensory modulation* is the ability to adjust the response to incoming sensory input. *Sensory discrimination* is the ability to differentiate, categorize, and interpret different sensory inputs. *Sensory-based motor processing* is the ability to use sensory input for motor output.

discrimination, and sensory-based motor processing.[8] These categories are important in understanding the complexity behind sensory processing.

Sensory modulation *is the brain's "ability to adjust the response to incoming sensory input in order to maintain an appropriate arousal level."*[1] Put simply, it is the ability to turn up or turn down the level of sensory input that is experienced.[9] It allows us to adjust the amount of sensory input we need in a particular moment in order to stay regulated. Intensity, frequency, and duration of a sensory input influences modulation. Modulation also allows for the habituation and sensitization of sensory input to prevent from getting flooded or overwhelmed, like we outlined in the dog barking example in the previous section. It helps a student to tune out the traffic noise outside the window when they are listening to the teacher, or ignore the tag in the back of their shirt so they can focus on their independent work. There are certain physiological, or body-based, responses associated with the modulation of sensory input based on how the input is influencing one's arousal level and state of regulation. Our heart rate may slow down or speed up, our breathing may become deeper or shallower, our body temperature may fall or rise. As a note, we all have different thresholds for certain inputs, which will be expounded upon in the next chapter. Movement of our body is also influenced by sensory modulation. We might cock our head and lean closer to listen to a quiet conversation. We might pull our hand away quickly when we touch something slimy and squishy. We might pucker our lips and open our eyes wide when we eat something sour.

Sensory discrimination *is the brain's "ability to differentiate one sensory input from another and interpret the meaning of that sensory input."*[1] Put simply, it is the ability to determine the difference between two inputs. This form of sensory processing focuses more on the details of a stimulus and helps us to categorize sensory inputs, such as hard versus soft (tactile), English versus Spanish (auditory), circle versus square (visual), and firm versus gentle (proprioceptive). It also helps us anticipate the properties of sensory inputs and associate meaning with sensory inputs. For example, the other day when Jamie reached into a bag of potatoes, she was anticipating a firm, rough, and slightly bumpy texture. To her surprise she felt a wet, mushy texture that caused her to quickly retract her hand and shriek—a rotten potato! It can be quite dysregulating, and maybe even stressful, when our expectations don't match our experience. Discrimination requires higher levels of the brain to be accessed, as it is more of a conscious process compared to modulation—it demands our attention.[6] Modulation, on the other hand, tends to occur without us thinking about it. Appropriate modulation of an input is generally a precursor to appropriate discrimination.[10] This is because the brain must be able to modulate sensory input in order to be in a regulated state which allows us to access the higher-level areas required for discrimination. If the brain is in a "fight, flight, or freeze" state, it does not care much about discerning the details of something.

Sensory-based motor processing *is the brain's "ability to utilize sensory input to produce a motor outcome."*[1] Put simply, it is how we use information from our internal senses to move our bodies. This is a more specialized form of processing that primarily integrates information from the tactile, proprioceptive, and vestibular systems. Sensory-based motor processing contributes to our ability to move in a coordinated, efficient manner; this includes moving our mouth to speak and eat, moving our hands to write and tie shoes, and moving our body to sit in a chair and climb. It also contributes to how we plan and organize our body movements and our space. As you will come to know, this area of sensory processing underlies many of the motor output requirements at school—especially in terms of confidence and competence. Chapter 8 is entirely devoted to these concepts.

While the appropriate modulation and discrimination of each individual sensory system is important for regulation and learning, the integration of all the sensory responses is what truly facilitates learning and doing. Yes, there are experiences and activities in which certain sensory inputs play a more dominant role. Yet we still rely on the complex interconnectedness of all our sensory systems to fully participate in those experiences. Remember, the sum of all our senses is greater than the individual parts. Multisensory learning experiences, both within and outside of the school environment, will yield stronger brain connections, more integrated brain activation, highly engaged and more successful learners.

Cultural Considerations with Sensory Processing

Culture invariably impacts how we experience and perceive the world around us. Research suggests, for example, that people from various cultures have differing abilities in perceiving smells. In a preliminary study that compared caregiver perceptions of sensory processing differences in children with and without Autism Spectrum Disorder (ASD), Israeli caregivers reported fewer unusual responses to sensory experiences in both typically developing children and children with ASD, as compared to US caregivers.[11] This suggests that there may be cultural variations in how caregivers perceive and report sensory processing differences; your view of what may be "normal" or "typical" may differ from that of someone who grew up in another culture or country. Emerging research also indicates that language around sensory perceptions can be limited in certain cultures, so communicating differences in sensory processing may be difficult.[12] Consequently, for educators in multi-cultural classrooms, the language that you use when communicating with caregivers about sensory processing may not translate exactly and may require additional understanding of the student's cultural background and experiences.

Because culture is embedded in one's environment, it can also influence how the nervous system responds to different sensory inputs. We know through research that the environment shapes our sensory experiences, such as babies who spend a significant amount of time in the NICU or children of any age who have stayed in an orphanage.[12,13] For example, a child raised in a quiet household who is expected to play peacefully with little background noise may prefer environments that are less noisy; however, a child raised in a boisterous house with extended family members always coming and going may prefer auditory input. Some cultures and families that highly value cleanliness may limit the interaction a child has with messy textures, such as playing with food, digging in the mud, or finger painting; this may cause the child to be hesitant to engage in these activities when presented with the opportunity outside of the home. Keep in mind that, because genetics and neurological development also impact responses to sensory input, there may be a mismatch between the sensory environment and the sensory needs of a child. This type of culture clash could potentially result in misunderstanding the child's behaviors or negatively influence the caregiver's (or teacher's) ability to co-regulate with the child. This will be touched on more in Chapter 3 when sensory preferences are discussed.

Admittedly there is still a lot we do not know about the influence of culture on how we process or perceive sensory input. To date research is very limited in this area. Even so, it's important to consider how a student's cultural background may influence their engagement with the sensory environment before making any assumptions. Know that your perceptions of sensory experiences may differ from those with different cultural backgrounds, and that unique cultures exist in every household as well. Some caregivers may raise concern about their child being "too wiggly" when completing homework; listen to their concern, don't brush it off as the child "just being a kid." Likewise, you may raise concern about a student touching too many things in the classroom, and the caregiver may see this as a cultural strength of using hands as a means of expression. As we've mentioned, maintaining an open and curious stance will help you remain in a regulated space that will allow you to learn more about a student's cultural background and his previous experiences, and how those experiences may be impacting his sensory processing, state of regulation, and engagement in the learning experience.

Incorporating Sensory Integration into the Classroom

Now that we have established the importance of sensory integration for learning, it is important to consider how to facilitate the use of sensory integration in the classroom. A balance of sensory stimulation is important for maintaining appropriate regulation of your students. Remember that certain sensory inputs are important in different situations; students may need more stimulation in the morning to "get going" and less stimulation at the end of the day to "de-stress." When coming back from recess or an assembly, students may need calming input to set the stage for learning again. You can refer to Figure 1.5 for examples of inputs that are more calming versus inputs that are more stimulating.

All behavior is a form of communication, and students tell us through their behaviors which sensory inputs are regulating and dysregulating to them. As adults, we need to be attuned enough to watch for and listen to what they are communicating. **Attunement**, *in short, means being*

Recognizing the difference between calming and alerting sensory inputs is an important step in understanding how you can help manage the regulation and behavior in your students simply by changing their environment. Look at the lists below and consider which sensory inputs would be beneficial at certain points in the school day.

Calming Sensory Inputs	Alerting Sensory Inputs
• Quiet, instrumental music • Lavender, chamomile, eucalyptus, and jasmine essential oils • Deep pressure inputs (hugs, body squeezes, weighted objects) • Rubbing a soft object • Chewy foods like gum, fruit leather, dried fruit, beef jerky, and granola bars • Rocking back and forth • Low lighting and natural sunlight • Slow, repeated visual stimulation (lava lamp, fish tank, starry globe) • Warm room temperature	• Loud, fast-paced music • Mint, orange, and cinnamon essential oils • Light touch (tickling, brushing against the skin, scratchy textures) • Sour and spicy foods like pickles, lemonade, sour candy, flaming Cheetos, Takis, and red hots • Spinning in a circle or going upside-down • Flourescent lights and direct sunlight • Fast, ever-changing visual stimulation (TV, videos, people moving around) • Cold room temperature

Sensory inputs I can use in the morning: _____

_____

Sensory inputs I can use after recess: _____

_____

Sensory inputs I can use at the end of the day: _____

_____

Taken from Chaves, J. & Taylor, A. (2020). *The "Why" Behind Classroom Behaviors: Integrative Strategies for Learning, Regulation, and Relationships.* Corwin: Thousand Oaks, CA.

Figure 1.5 Influence of Sensory Input on Behavior

attentive, responsive, and understanding.[1] Look for a student's cues to better understand what they are trying to communicate. Always remember to ask questions about why a student is responding in a certain way. It may be beneficial for you to think back to your preschool, elementary, or junior high classroom and recall the sensory environment. Was there a class pet that brought a strong odor to the room? Did the teacher like to play music in the background? Were the chairs hard and uncomfortable? Now think about your current classroom as a teacher. What artwork and posters are on the walls? Is there natural light from the windows? How often do students get up to move around? Are there sensory experiences that students often complain about?

Given that sensory processing influences our state of regulation and is integral to our learning, utilizing activities that facilitate sensory integration will be beneficial for all the students in your classroom. "When a student has strong sensory integration that produces efficient motor movements, engaged social interaction, and effective regulation, learning can then be maximized."[1] You may already use some of these in your classroom, such as hands-on teaching activities, Go Noodle® videos as movement breaks, and listening to an audiobook while following along in a book. Are there ways you can incorporate more of them throughout the day? Are there ways you can add variety to the sensory experiences to help the brain grow even more?

This is a good time to talk about structure and setting appropriate classroom expectations. There are many other resources out there, and even entire books devoted to this concept, so we won't go into too much detail. Yet we do want to point out that students do best when there is a balance of consistency, routines, and predictability while still being understanding, supportive, and responsive to individual needs.[1] All students require guidelines and expectations that are presented clearly so that students know what is being asked of them. This type of consistency is required in order for students to feel safe, in control and regulated. The key is finding the balance between holding the structure and expectations within the confines of a safe, regulating relationship.[1] Students will be more likely to engage in the lesson and follow directions if they feel connected with their teacher. They will be motivated to maintain a positive relationship with their teacher if they feel positively towards their teacher. There are ways to hold and maintain boundaries and expectations while also scaffolding students. This results in recognizing and celebrating a student's individual differences while also providing them with opportunities to reach their potential in a safe and consistent environment.[1] This is true with sensory input as well. Students should be allowed to access different sensory tools and sensory inputs when needed, while following the guidelines and expectations delineated by the teacher. We want to recognize that certain students will require more or less sensory input than others. We want to recognize that your entire class may demonstrate the need for more or less sensory input at certain times of day, but the type of sensory input and way in which you provide the sensory input matters. Keep this in mind while reading through the strategies below.

One way to help with sensory integration is to *celebrate movement* in the classroom by allowing students the opportunity to move around.[1] When a child's movement is restricted, this also restricts the activation of the vestibular sense, which is what contributes to attention and arousal.[1] This can often result in fidgeting, inattention, poor motivation, and dysregulation. By allowing students the opportunity to move around the classroom and explore things hands-on, you are helping them to activate their vestibular sense. Brain Breaks® and movement activities are an effective way to integrate movement and touch into the classroom on a regular basis in order to help students learn more about themselves, learn more about their environment, and better integrate the information learned during the lesson plan. Research indicates that, when students are provided with more movement

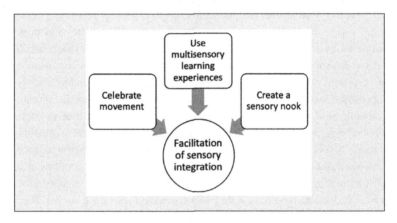

Figure 1.6 Ways to Facilitate Sensory Integration in the Classroom

Engaging all of the sensory systems in the classroom can facilitate improved integration in the brain, which will result in more engaged learning.

opportunities during lesson plans and at recess, attention during the lesson improves, academic outcomes improve, behavior improves, and stress is reduced.[15,16] Appendix A can serve as a guide to get you started on integrating more movement into your classroom in an effective manner. Incorporating these movement opportunities into your school day will allow your students to be more productive and engaged learners in the long run. Inserting a movement-based activity in between periods of focused attention can help to "reset" your students' brains and bodies for improved learning. Try adding just one or two activities per day to start with and slowly work up to integrating three to five movement opportunities per day.

Keep in mind that celebrating movement does not mean amping up students. There is certainly a balance of using movement to help students refocus and get back to a calm, alert state while making sure they don't get so overstimulated that it's challenging for them to sit back down to learn. This is where your attunement to your students comes into play. If you notice that a particular student seems to get too amped up after movement breaks and has difficulty refocusing on schoolwork, try a movement break that is more calming to his nervous system (like yoga poses) or try stopping the movement break two minutes early to do a calming activity (like deep breathing) that resets the stage for attentive learning. In addition, understanding the developmental expectations of attention for students at certain ages is helpful in knowing what to ask of your students. This will help to manage your own expectations of how long students can sustain attention, and will also help to decrease your own frustration as well as the frustration of your students.[1]

Another great strategy to facilitate sensory integration is by *using multisensory learning experiences* to bring different sensory elements into everyday classroom lessons and activities[1]. In this way you can "not only enhance your students' integration of sensory input but also enhance their learning experiences."[1] We can embrace the fact that all students learn differently and use this to our advantage. Traditional classroom instruction tends to favor auditory and visual inputs, yet tactile (touch), vestibular (movement), and proprioceptive (body awareness) inputs are just as important for making new neural connections. There are many creative ways in which multisensory activities can be utilized in the curriculum. You may even be using many of these currently, such as acting out a scene in a play, using manipulatives to learn addition and subtraction, or drawing maps in social studies. Appendix B has many examples, sorted by subject area, to get you

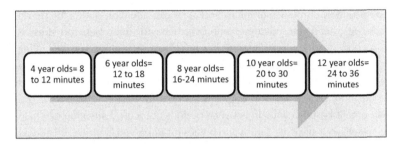

4 year olds= 8 to 12 minutes

6 year olds= 12 to 18 minutes

8 year olds= 16-24 minutes

10 year olds= 20 to 30 minutes

12 year olds= 24 to 36 minutes

Figure 1.7 Age-Appropriate Attention Spans

It is important to know the age-appropriate sustained attention spans for your students so that your expectations match developmental expectations. Knowing developmentally appropriate attention spans may help reduce your frustration and enhance your understanding of your students' needs, ultimately helping you to be more regulated as well. Inserting a movement-based activity in between periods of attending can help to "reset' your students' brains and bodies for improved learning.

Taken from Chaves, J., & Taylor, A. (2020). *The "Why" Behind Classroom Behaviors: Integrative Strategies for Learning, Regulation, and Relationships.* Thousand Oaks, CA: Corwin.

started or to help you build on what you're already doing. The activities in Appendix B are ways to enhance learning experiences and facilitate a more integrated, regulated brain for all of your students. At first, integrating such strategies into your class and curriculum may feel overwhelming or implausible, but don't worry. You can do it! In fact, including just one multisensory learning opportunity per class period will do wonders for your students and also help to keep you more regulated as a teacher.

Finally, consider *creating a sensory nook* to provide a calming space for students to reregulate when needed.[1] Given the large amount of sensory stimulation present throughout a school day, it is important to allow students the space to explore soothing sensory experiences. These calm experiences also facilitate a more integrated brain by keeping the sympathetic and parasympathetic nervous systems in balance.[1] This will, in turn, allow the student to better engage in the learning process and access higher level thinking. If, initially, students need to use the sensory nook more frequently, that's OK as long as you outline specific guidelines and expectations for its use. As students receive appropriate scaffolding for academics, adjust to the learning environment, and are provided appropriate sensory accommodations, they will start to feel safe and regulated on a more frequent basis; in turn, they will require less use of the calming sensory nook.[1]

- When should a student use the sensory nook? There can be many indicators that a student needs a calm space to reregulate. Here are a few:[1]

    - Difficulty with attending to the task at-hand that is negatively impacting the learning experience (for either that student or the students around them)

    - Transitioning into the classroom or between activities in the classroom is challenging for the student

    - The student is displaying behaviors that are out of the norm for that student, suggesting increased dysregulation for any number of reasons (e.g. not enough sleep, did not eat breakfast, dad left on a business trip, mom just had a baby, etc.)

    - Emotional dysregulation is being displayed in the form of crying, using vulgar language, throwing things, hitting others, and self-injurious behaviors

    - The student specifically requests to use the space

    - The student seems unusually quiet, or withdrawn, disengaged, or sad

- What should a sensory nook include? The answer here depends on the space you have available and the specific needs of students. In general we recommend the following[1]:

    - Comfortable seating, such as large pillows, bean bag chairs, or a padded rocking chair

    - A tent or canopy to minimize the amount of fluorescent light in the area (or you can simply remove the fluorescent light tube from above the sensory nook)

    - Opportunities to engage the proprioceptive system, such as stress balls, squishy pillows, geoboard with rubber bands, chalkboards with chalk, and/or a donut therapy ball

    - Noise-cancelling headphones to filter out auditory input

- Calming visual opportunities like picture books, a glitter jar, and/ or a fish tank (real or LED-based)
- A visual schedule and an image of the Zones of Regulation® to help facilitate communication with the child and an understanding of the child's state of arousal

These ways to promote sensory integration will be beneficial for all students in your classroom. They will help facilitate improved regulation, increased brain connectivity, and more attentive listening—all of which will augment their capacity for more complex thinking and learning.[1] Recall that sensory input serves as building blocks for all other learning, so investing time in laying good multisensory foundations will go a long way. In the next chapter we will discuss the dynamic relationship between regulation and sensory processing to help you better

Figure 1.8 Creating a Sensory Nook

A sensory nook is a safe space, with a variety of calming sensory inputs, where students can go in order to reregulate before engaging in the learning process. When a student is more regulated they will be better able to take in information and access higher cognitive skills.

Taken from Chaves, J., & Taylor, A. (2020). *The "Why" Behind Classroom Behaviors: Integrative Strategies for Learning, Regulation, and Relationships.* Thousand Oaks, CA: Corwin.

identify when students may require use of these strategies, and to better understand how regulation influences a student's ability to participate in school-based activities.

References

1. Chaves, J., & Taylor, A. (2020). *The "Why" Behind Classroom Behaviors: Integrated Strategies for Learning, Regulation, and Relationships.* Thousand Oaks, CA: Corwin.

2. Lewis, M. D., & Todd, R. M. (2007). The self-regulating brain: Cortical-subcortical feedback and the development of intelligent action. *Cognitive Development, 22*(4), 406–430.

3. Doidge, N. (2007). *The Brain that Changes Itself: Stories of Personal Triumph from the Frontiers of Brain Science.* New York: Penguin.

4. Paolicellim, R. C., Bolasco, G., Pagani, F., Maggi, L., Scianni, M., Panzanelli, P., … & Gross, C. (2011). Synaptic pruning by microglia is necessary for normal brain development. *Science, 333*(6048), 1456–1458.

5. Siegel, D. J. (2012). *The Developing Mind: How Relationships and the Brain Interact to Shape Who We Are* (2nd ed.). New York: Guilford Press.

6. Burpee, J. (2015). *Sensory Integrative Intensive Continuing Education Course.* Medfield, MA: Educational Resources, Inc.

7. Gainsley, S. (2011). Look, listen, touch, feel, taste: The importance of sensory play. *Highscope Extensions, 25*(5), 1–5.

8. Miller, L. J., Anzalone, M. E., Lane, S. J, Cermak, S. A., & Osten, E. T. (2007). Concept evolution in sensory integration: A proposed nosology for diagnosis. *American Journal of Occupational Therapy, 61*(2), 135–140.

9. Ayers, A. J. (2005). *Sensory Integration and the Child: Understanding Hidden Sensory Challenges.* Los Angeles, CA: Western Psychological Services.

10. Case-Smith, J., Allen, A. S., & Pratt, P. N. (2001). *Occupational Therapy for Children* (6th ed.). St. Louis, MO: Mosby.

11. Caron, K. G., Schaaf, R. C., Benevides, T. W., & Gal, E. (2012). Cross-cultural comparison of sensory behaviors in children with autism. *American Journal of Occupational Therapy, 66*(5), e77–e80.

12. Caballero, R., & Paradis, C. (2015). Making sense of sensory perceptions across languages and cultures. *Functions of Language, 22*(1), 1–19.

13. Broring, T., Konigs, M., Oostrom, K. J., Lafeber, H. N., Brugman, A., & Oosterlaan, J. (2018). Sensory processing difficulties in school-age children born very preterm: An exploratory study. *Early Human Development, 117*, 22–31.

14. Pineda, R., Guth, R., Herring, A., Reynolds, L., Oberle, S., & Smith, J. (2017). Enhancing sensory experiences for very preterm infants in the NICU: An integrative review. *Journal of Perinatology: Official Journal of the California Perinatal Association, 37*(4), 323–332. doi:10.1038/jp.2016.179

15. Hanscom, A. (2016). *Balanced and Barefoot: How Unrestricted Outdoor Play Makes for Strong, Confident, and Capable Children*. Oakland, CA: New Harbinger Publications.

16. Norris, E., van Steen, T., Direito, A., & Stamatakis, E. (2019). Physically active lessons in schools and their impact on physical activity, educational, health and cognition outcomes: A systematic review and meta-analysis. *British Journal of Sports Medicine*. Advance online publication. doi:10.1136/bjsports-2018–100502

2 The Connection between Sensory Processing, Regulation, and Relationships

We've discussed the brain and nervous system as well as established the importance of sensory processing for regulation and participation in learning. We can now dive deeper into the connection between regulation, relationships, and sensory processing. As we've mentioned, **regulation** *is an individual's ability to manage his or her internal emotional and physical state in order to stay calm and engaged.* When students are regulated they are able to access the part of their brain that allows them to maintain an optimal state of arousal, which supports their ability to sustain attention and remain engaged in the learning process.[1] Students who are not in a regulated state often display behaviors that communicate to us that something is wrong. Rather than penalizing or punishing students for these behaviors, we, as the adults in their lives, need to recognize that the behaviors are coming from a dysregulated state. We need to figure out how to support students in becoming regulated so that they can maximize their engagement in learning. One way to do this is by better understanding how sensory input may be causing students and teachers to become dysregulated.

Redefining Behavior as Communication

While what we typically view as disruptive behaviors often appear as though students are trying to get attention or be manipulative, in reality, these behaviors are, more often than not, a student's attempt to communicate to us that something is wrong or off balance. An underlying factor is causing the student's brain and nervous system to enter into a state of dysregulation. As supportive adults in their lives, it is our job to dig a little deeper, to discern what they are communicating through the behavior, and ultimately help them to reach a state of regulation so that they can better access the parts of their brain that allow them to learn.[1] This often takes time and can sometimes even be a bit frustrating. It requires your attention and attunement, and it also requires you to be in a regulated state yourself. When we as adults are feeling dysregulated, we are less able to attend to the needs of others, and we may be more irritable or disengaged, which will disrupt our own ability to problem solve appropriately.

As teachers, and those of us who work with children, it can be helpful to take a moment to examine our own thoughts and beliefs about behaviors. When a student is misbehaving, how do you view this misbehavior? What thoughts or sayings pop into your mind? Do you think, "this student is being manipulative, or just trying to get attention"? Do you blame bad parenting? Do you take the misbehavior personally and feel as though the student is doing this intentionally to make you mad? Do you think "I need to ask more questions to find out what may be underlying this behavior"?

Interestingly, the way in which you interpret your student's behavior may be impacted by your own state of regulation, and it will undoubtedly impact the way you respond. A *shift in your state of regulation* can change the way you interpret and respond to your student's behavior. Additionally, *a shift in your interpretation* of the behavior can make all the difference not only to your student's day, but also to your student's life and academic success.

This shift allows one to move away from blaming and shaming the student (or their caregivers) for the behavior that is seen, towards a better understanding of what is underlying the behavior. If you notice your mind thinking this student is being manipulative or attention-seeking, pause, and wonder, "what is this student trying to communicate to me?" Is the student responding to something in the environment that is overwhelming or underwhelming them to the point where their brain is not in a receptive place? What sensory input in the environment is impacting *my* state of regulation and impacting *my* ability to engage thoughtfully with my students? Why might a particular student, or a few students, always seem to be reprimanded? Instead of falling back on the same behavior management tactics that you are used to, take a moment instead to explore what is underlying the behavior. There are many factors that contribute to changes in regulation in students and teachers. In this book we focus on how sensory input may be underlying the behavioral challenges we see in school and how to better allow you, as teachers, and your students, to maintain or regain a state of regulation in order to optimize learning.

Being able to shift our awareness to how sensory input impacts our state of regulation and that of our students can guide our reactions, responses, and behavioral management in our classrooms. If the sound of a particular student's voice triggers us, we may respond more harshly to them than to other students. If a student enjoys exploring things with their hands yet you highly value organization and order, you may become annoyed with them messing things up rather than joining in with their curiosity. If, for example, you notice you become more detached towards the end of the day perhaps the sensory input from the day has caused you to become fatigued, impacting your ability to maintain a warm, inviting stance. Bring awareness to your patterns of regulation and how sensory input can impact your state of regulation; this will also ultimately impact your teaching style and how you connect with students throughout the day.

We have observed programs that attempt to integrate sensory-based and social-emotional strategies, and despite their best efforts, they lose too much structure and become too permissive, resulting in students displaying even more behavioral problems than before.[1] Know that it is OK to hold students accountable for their behaviors, while also providing them with appropriate support in a relationally safe environment. One way to understand this concept in a simple way—which you can also use to explain to students—is that *there are no "bad" or wrong feelings, however, not all behaviors are OK.*[1] It is OK to get agitated at not being able to move around in your chair, for example, but it is not OK to get up and wander around the room while the teacher is talking. It is OK to become frustrated with the visual information from an entire page of math problems in front of you, but it is not OK to run out of the room while throwing your math paper on the ground. It is OK to become overwhelmed when there is too much noise, but it is not OK to hit the peer next to you for talking too loudly. It is OK to feel discouraged when you've attempted, unsuccessfully, to cut along the lines of an art project, but it is not OK to start cutting the paper into tiny pieces and throw them in the air like confetti. Remember, when you are seeing behaviors such as these, to keep sensory input in mind. Using the examples above, think of ways you can provide scaffolding to students so they can regain a state of regulation in a way that is appropriate for your classroom setting as well as teach them the skills they need in order to be successful.

A student may be having difficulty processing or integrating certain sensory input which is impacting their behavior, and ultimately impacting their ability to maintain regulation, attention, and learning. If a student is exhibiting disruptive behaviors, or withdrawn behaviors, this likely means that there is a skill they are lacking that impacts their ability to meet the demands, or the expectations, of the classroom. What sensory input may be impacting their ability to meet the demands of the classroom? What sensory input is impacting their state of regulation, which also ultimately impacts their ability to learn? These are questions we hope you will find answers to in the remaining pages of this book.

Dysregulation can take many forms. As noted, "acting out" or "disruptive" behaviors can be signs of dysregulation. These may include running away, hiding under a desk, yelling, hitting a peer, banging one's head, or refusal to participate. But there are many students struggling with dysregulation who aren't necessarily exhibiting these externalized behaviors. Rather, they internalize feelings of dysregulation which can look like boredom, sluggishness, anxiety, carelessness, a lack of engagement, or wanting to be alone.[1] Both types of behaviors—overt and covert—are ways the student communicates that they are not regulated. Dysregulation underlying both externalized and internalized behaviors may indicate that a student is having difficulty integrating and processing certain types of sensory information. Sometimes a student may know what triggered the dysregulation, but oftentimes a student may not know. The upcoming chapters will delineate common sensory-related signs teachers can look for that can be indications of sensory processing differences underlying the student's dysregulation.

A Cyclical Relationship between Sensory Processing and Regulation

Many things can influence one's state of regulation: lack of sleep, hunger or thirst, environmental stressors, learning challenges, performance anxiety, to name a few. For the sake of this book we focus on the influence of sensory processing. There is a dynamic relationship between our state of regulation and sensory processing, whereby each can influence the other both positively and negatively.

Let's first look at how sensory input influences our emotional state of regulation. The way in which we process emotions and experiences

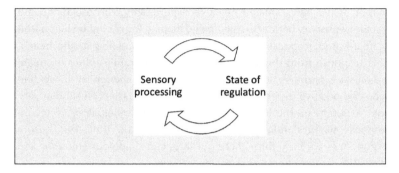

Figure 2.1 Cycle of Sensory Processing and Regulation

Sensory input—and the way in which we process that sensory input—has a dynamic relationship with our state of regulation. Sensory input can influence our state of regulation and our state of regulation can influence the way in which we process sensory input. It is important to hold these two concepts in mind as you consider the behaviors of your students.

is intrinsically intertwined with how we process the sensory information around us. This is because the emotional center of our brain—the amygdala—detects threat and safety based on the sensory information it is receiving (like we explored in the examples of the dog barking and the sea cucumber in Chapter 1).[2] A loud, blaring sound like a honking horn puts our amygdala on high alert because of the threat of a car coming. We need to engage our fight or flight system to act quickly to avoid getting hit. We stop any social interaction and are not interested in learning anything new. A soothing, gentle sound like a mother's voice singing a lullaby puts the amygdala at ease because it detects safety and comfort. This facilitates a regulated state that allows us to engage socially by smiling and singing along, as well as an opportunity to reflect on the day or think about the next day's activities. Both of these responses are useful and adaptive; both help us navigate the world and keep our bodies safe.

Recall from Chapter 1 that the amygdala "remembers" emotional responses from past sensory experiences, which has an impact on how we engage with repeated sensory experiences. The brain draws upon those memories when we face similar experiences in the future. This is how the brain learns to wire itself in a certain way (i.e. neuroplasticity)—and why we feel certain emotions with different sensory input or motor output. If we had repeated negative experiences with touching sand (tactile sensory experience), the amygdala may trigger an anxiety-based or fear-based response when someone suggests going to the beach. This response from the amygdala impairs the brain's ability to create a cohesive narrative and make sense of the experience. If we had repeated positive experiences with riding rollercoasters (vestibular sensory experience), the amygdala may trigger an anticipatory or secure response when standing in line at a theme park. Thus, the sensory experiences we have throughout our lives can shape our emotions and regulation around future sensory experiences.

Similarly, our state of regulation also influences how we perceive sensory information.[1] When we are in a calm or playful state, we can typically endure more sensory input than when we are in an anxious or fearful state. This is because, as we touched on previously, stress hormones (adrenaline and cortisol) shift the amygdala into a state of "high alert," thus increasing the response to threat and fear. The increased vigilance of the amygdala, in turn, makes sensory information more salient.[3] In this instance our senses are also heightened in order to engage in a fight, flight, or freeze response and keep us more aware of our environment. Some people, for example, may like hugs or cuddling the majority of the time because they are in a calm state of regulation. But when they become stressed due to workload, the political climate, the daily grind, or family illness they may find themselves wanting more space and getting annoyed when someone touches them. Other people, for example, may enjoy listening to music and can tolerate a fair range of volumes while still remaining regulated. Yet after a stressful day at work or caring for children they may find themselves getting frustrated with music in the background (at any volume) and request that it be turned off completely.

For a student, they may be able to maintain their attention to silent reading time despite the room being a little too hot. But if they just returned from recess where they were excluded from a game with peers or just found out that morning that they were moving away, they may become more agitated by the room temperature and lose focus easily. When an activity is meaningful and motivating to a student, you may notice that they are not as impacted by the sensory environment. A student who really enjoys art may be fully engaged in creating a map of the United States even though the sound of construction vehicles is booming outside the classroom. Yet 15 minutes prior, when the teacher was discussing important geographical landmarks in the United States, they seemed to turn and look outside the window every time they heard a loud noise. As you can see, stress on the nervous system can, at times, be compounded by sensory input. Other times that stress can be managed by engaging in meaningful activities despite the sensory environment. However, not all stress is created equal.

A Note about Stress

Research demonstrates that some degree of stress can be adaptive.[4] Adaptive stress results in brief increases in heart rate and mild elevations in stress hormones, which often motivates us to change, learn, and get things done. Once the stressful event is over our heart rate decreases, as does the elevation in our stress hormones. Sometimes stress reaches a point where we need the support of someone from a positive, protective relationship— this is called tolerable stress.[4] In these situations, we experience a serious, but temporary, stress response that is buffered and mitigated by a safe, trusting relationship so that our heart rate and stress hormones return to "baseline," or normal, after the stressor is over.

Toxic stress responses, however, occur when there is a prolonged activation of the stress response with no protective relationships.[4] This results in one's heart rate and stress hormones constantly remaining at an elevated level.[5] Toxic stress can result in long-term physical and mental health complications, including the inability to properly integrate sensory experiences.[5] When we experience toxic stress, we cannot appropriately access the higher levels of our brain over an extended of time. Trauma and systemic racism can also lead to toxic stress, which can impede the brain's ability to process and integrate sensory information. Additionally, repeated negative sensory and sensorimotor experiences can lead to the development of toxic stress. This is what may happen to students with sensory processing disorder (SPD), if their distress signs are ignored and their needs are unaddressed. Chapter 3 will talk more in-depth about SPD.

Thresholds for the different levels of stress will, of course, be different for all students depending on their individual needs, previous experiences, and nervous system responses. Giving a speech in front of the class, taking a test, or writing an essay, for example, likely cause levels of adaptive stress for most students. For other students, who may have a learning difference or an SPD,

31

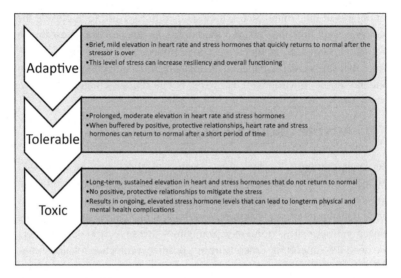

Figure 2.2 Levels of Stress

Stress can be defined as adaptive, tolerable, or toxic. The level of stress experienced by a student will impact their ability to engage in activities within the school environment. Positive, protective relationships can buffer the effects of stress, helping a student get back to a state of regulation in order to access higher cognitive levels of the brain needed for problem solving, organization, self-control, and sustained attention, to name a few.

Adapted from Harvard University Center on the Developing Child. Toxic Stress. Retrieved from https://developingchild.harvard.edu/science/key-concepts/toxic-stress/ (Accessed August 2020).

these activities may cause a tolerable level of stress if they have supportive and protective relationships in their lives. Unfortunately, for students who may have experienced trauma, systemic racism, or who have no protective relationships, such academic activities may cause toxic levels of stress.

One way to begin a simple shift in our interpretation of students' behavior is understanding how they react to levels of stress. We can often tell what stress level our student is experiencing by "listening" closely to their non-verbal cues and better understanding the source of their behaviors. While adaptive levels of stress can help build resilience, frustration tolerance, confidence, and adaptation to new situations, toxic stress can cause not only what looks like disruptive or "manipulative" behaviors but it can also actually disrupt brain development and cause long-term physical health complications. Luckily, we know that positive, supportive, relationships are a powerful way in which stress can be mitigated.[6]

The Impact of Co-Regulation on Sensory Processing

The relationship between state of regulation and sensory input is important because, as you know, we move through different states of regulation and different sensory environments throughout the day.[1] We may be calm, relaxed, happy, and ready to focus at one moment, or stressed, angry, and frustrated at another. We may be in a quiet room sitting at a desk with little visual input on the walls and then transition to a loud, odorous cafeteria with people moving around everywhere. Still, we often have strategies to move back into a state of calm when we get dysregulated. Sometimes these strategies involve use of sensory input, such as squeezing our fists, rubbing a soft object, or chewing a piece of gum, and sometimes this means more brain-based strategies such as taking a deep breath, engaging in self-talk, or brief meditation. When we cannot achieve regulation ourselves then we often look to others around us to help with co-regulation.

For students who experience additional stress in the classroom, related to sensory processing differences or other learning differences, a positive relationship with the teacher can serve as a buffer to creating negative neural pathways and facilitate positive learning experiences.[1] This is really good news because it means that students who are struggling in the classroom, who may be disengaged or misbehaving, can get to a more regulated state in order to access the higher cognitive areas of the brain through their relationship with you! This, in turn, helps rewire the connections in their brain over time to be more successful in school and less reactive to the sensory environment and/or academic curriculum. Building positive, integrated connections through safe, regulated experiences is therefore one of the most essential things you can do as a teacher.

Establishing a positive teacher–student relationship highly influences how a student engages in learning. We know that because of certain processes in the brain (such as mirror neurons), emotions and states of regulation can be contagious.[7] Emotional states of teachers can "rub off" on students. The reverse is also true: a dysregulated student can negatively impact a teacher's state of regulation. Developing an awareness of the interconnectedness between your state of regulation and that of your students will help you better reach a state of co-regulation. **Co-regulation** *is the "attuned and responsive interactions between a child (student) and adult (teacher) that allow them to reach a state of regulation together."*[1] This is critical for students who are experiencing difficulty self-regulating in certain situations, such as those with an SPD. This is also crucial for students who have experienced systemic racism and may not have positive associations with teachers or authority figures. As we already explored, regulation is an essential foundation for a feeling of safety in order to access higher brain functions for learning. Consequently, a co-regulated state is optimal for learning.

One way to be "that person" who is able to provide a supportive, co-regulated relationships with your students is by coming alongside them. Can you think of a student who is disruptive, angry, isolated, or withdrawn? What do you know about their history and who is there for them? From what we've discussed about the brain and how toxic levels of stress can be mitigated by just one supportive, protective relationship, how can you join with them to support their needs? What questions do you need to keep asking to uncover why they may be demonstrating certain behaviors?

"Research clearly shows that our brains are influenced by the relationships and experiences we have with others"[1]—for better or for worse. In addition to safe relationships with others, adequate sensory opportunities and predictable environments yield more brain integration for developing children.[6,8-9] Forming safe, trusting relationships in sensory-attuned environments can therefore influence the development, growth, and integration of a student's brain. While this can be challenging at times, it is important to focus on the quality of the relationship you have with all your students. If you are curious to learn more ways in which you can facilitate co-regulation with your students there are many resources that you may find useful, such as *The "Why" Behind Classroom Behaviors,*[1] *The Whole-Brain Child,*[6] *Beyond Behaviors,*[10] and *Lost at School.*[11]

There may be times when you are co-regulating with a student without realizing it. Your calm, trusting, understanding presence may oftentimes be enough for students. It is the language you use: "I understand you're having a hard time. Let's figure it out together," and the nonverbal messages you send. It is important not to assume that a student is acting a certain way because of laziness, defiance, lack of concern, or boredom. When you look at behaviors as a form of communication, this facilitates the engagement in a co-regulatory relationship in order to get the student back to a regulated state[1]. Once in a regulated state, you can talk with the student about what may be challenging for them in order to problem solve and re-engage them in the learning process.

Co-regulation can also influence the way in which a student responds to sensory input and sensorimotor activities. The feeling of safety can increase the student's neurological capacity for otherwise stressful sensory experiences, turning them into something more manageable.[1] This ultimately allows the student to better explore and engage in an activity that will facilitate learning. For example, a student may sit next to you during a loud assembly in order to feel safe and later report that they really enjoyed the presentation. The reverse is also true. The feeling of threat or fear from someone else can exacerbate the sensory experience and cause even more distress on the nervous system. This further impedes the ability of higher brain areas to be accessed for engagement and learning. For example, a student who is told they need to focus more and try harder when using scissors to cut along the lines may have increased levels of stress, in turn causing the challenging activity to be even more difficult because they do not have the appropriate sensorimotor skills to do so. Conversely if the teacher helped the student with placing their fingers in the scissors and calmly stood next to the student, providing assistance when needed, the student would feel more regulated and better equipped to complete the task.

Because co-regulation plays such a powerful role in establishing a safe, positive learning environment, your regulation as a teacher is vitally important. It is important to continuously check in with your own state of regulation throughout the day so that you have a better capacity to co-regulate with your students. Consider the following questions to reflect on your own regulation:[1]

- What times of day do I feel drained?
- What times of day do I feel restored?
- What are signs of dysregulation that I feel in myself?
- Who can I talk with to process the events of the day?
- What can I do to feel more regulated at school?
- Who are students who tend to trigger me?

• What sensory inputs overwhelm me?

• What sensory inputs are calming to me?

All this to say that your presence as a teacher can either positively or nega-tively influence the way in which a student explores and engages with the sensory environment. In the next chapter we will explore more ways in which sensory preferences impact your state of regulation, as well as the regulation of your students. Because classrooms contain a wide variety of sensory inputs, as we will explore more thoroughly in subsequent chapters, your co-regulation with students who have difficulty processing certain sensory inputs can actually increase their capacity to learn. Additionally, your recognition of times when you feel overstimulated by sensory input due to your sensory preferences will increase your capacity to co-regulate with students. When students feel threatened, unsafe, or uncertain in the classroom, they may become either more aware of the sights, sounds, smells, and tactile experiences through a heightened level of arousal, or less engaged with sights, sounds, smells, and tactile experiences by "zoning out" or "shutting down." Sensory input, therefore, may be one of the under-lying reasons causing a student to feel unsafe, dysregulated, or threatened. This happens to teachers as well; your ability to model regulation with awareness and sensitivity to sensory input will create opportunities for your students to develop regulation as well. You may find that some students need even more sensory-based support in school. The next chapter will delineate sensory processing disorders in order to help you better identify when a student may need additional accommodations and resources.

References

1. Chaves, J., & Taylor, A. (2020). *The "Why" Behind Classroom Behaviors: Integrated Strategies for Learning, Regulation, and Relationships.* Thousand Oaks, CA: Corwin.

2. Kranowitz, C. S. (2005). *The Out-of-Sync Child: Recognizing and Coping with Sensory Processing Disorder.* New York: Penguin Group.

3. van Marle, H. J., Hermans, E. J., Qin, S., & Fernández, G. (2009). From specifi-city to sensitivity: How acute stress affects amygdala processing of biologically salient stimuli. *Biological Psychiatry*, 66(7), 649–655.

4. Harvard University Center on the Developing Child. (n.d.). Toxic stress. Retrieved from https://developingchild.harvard.edu/science/key-concepts/toxic-stress/ (Accessed August 2020).

5. Van der Kolk, B. A. (2015). *The Body Keeps the Score: Brain, Mind, and Body in the Healing of Trauma.* New York: Penguin Books.

6. Siegel, D. J., & Payne Bryson, T. (2011). The Whole-Brain Child: 12 Revolutionary Strategies to Nurture Your Child's Developing Mind. New York: Bantam Books.

7. Iacoboni, M. (2008). *Mirroring People: The Science of Empathy and How We Connect with Others.* London: Picador.

8. Bick, J. B., Zhu, T., Stamoulis, C., Fox, N. A., Zeanah, C., & Nelson, C. A. (2015). Effect of early institutionalization and foster care on long-term white matter development: A randomized clinical trial. *JAMA Pediatrics, 169*(3), 211–219.

9. Perry, B. D. (2004). *Maltreated Children: Experience, Brain Development, and the Next Generation.* New York: W. W. Norton.

10. Delahooke, M (2019). *Beyond Behaviors: Using Brain Science and Compassion to Understand and Solve Children's Behavioral Challenges.* Eau Claire, WI: PESI.

11. Greene, R. W. (2009). *Lost at School: Why Our Kids with Behavioral Challenges Are Falling through the Cracks and How We Can Help Them.* New York: Simon & Schuster.

3 | Identifying Sensory Processing Disorder in the School Environment

We all process sensory inputs on a daily, hourly, minute-to-minute, basis but the way in which we process those inputs differs from person to person. Sometimes this can lead to a sensory processing disorder (SPD) whereby the sensory information is not being appropriately processed or integrated. As of 2007, an estimated 5–16% of children have SPD, with boys at a higher prevalence than girls.[1] Reports suggest that nearly 90% of children with Autism Spectrum Disorder (ASD) also have SPD.[2] With the incidence of ASD climbing from 1 in 110 in 2006 to 1 in 54 in 2016, it seems likely that the percentage of children with SPD is higher than the 2007 estimates.[3] There is also a 40–60% co-occurrence of ADHD and SPD, as well as a 17–35% co-occurrence of giftedness with SPD.[4,5] Anecdotally, teachers report a higher prevalence of students with suspected SPD in their classrooms as compared with five years ago. This is particularly reflected in fidgeting behaviors, slouched posture, and difficulty with visual attention. What all these numbers indicate is that there is a high likelihood that at least a handful of students in your classroom will benefit from sensory-based accommodations. This starts with your ability to recognize SPD in your students. Let's first delineate the difference between sensory preferences and an SPD.

Impact of Sensory Preferences

Everyone experiences certain preferences for sensory inputs that influence our state of regulation. Some inputs help us become more regulated while others can result in dysregulation. Your **sensory preferences** *impact "how you take in information, whether you tend to be more extroverted or introverted, your learning style, and the activities in which you engage.* We tend to shy away from sensory input that is more challenging for us to process and lean into sensory input that we process more readily."[6] Sometimes these preferences are influenced by our environment, while others are influenced by our genetics. It's not uncommon for one caregiver to relate better to the sensory needs of his or her child compared to the other caregiver or for a teacher to relate better to the sensory needs of one student compared to another. What's important to know is that these sensory preferences generally do not result in a maladaptive fight, flight, or freeze response, but they can influence one's regulation.[6]

Consider what sensory inputs may be impacting your own state of regulation throughout the school day. Do you become drained after being in a loud auditorium? Do you feel restored after having a quiet break, or a warm cup of tea or coffee? Do you become easily frustrated when navigating new motor experiences, like setting up a projector? Do you feel comforted when a fellow teacher gives you a hug in the break room? Just as we are constantly impacted by the sensory input from our environment, the students that we work with are as well.

Understanding your own emotional responses to sensory input can not only increase your awareness around regulation but also increase your ability to relate to students' responses to sensory inputs.[6] What sensory inputs support your regulation and ability to engage adaptively with the world around you? What sensory inputs cause you to become dysregulated and negatively impact how you engage with your students? If there is a mismatch between your sensory preferences and the sensory input in the environment, you will likely experience some degree of stress. Decreasing the stress you feel can facilitate improved co-regulation with your students, ultimately enhancing your teaching abilities and their learning experience.

Consider:

- Which visual, auditory, touch, smell, taste, and movement sensory experiences cause you to become *more dysregulated*?

- Which visual, auditory, touch, smell, taste, and movement sensory experiences cause you to achieve a *better state of regulation*?

- How are these responses similar or different to students in your class?
- How do these responses change depending on other stressors: lack of sleep, hunger, illness, family dynamics, political climate, financial state?

There may be some activities that you do on a frequent basis to help achieve a better state of regulation or help increase your focus. There may be some activities that consistently cause a state of dysregulation, so you try to avoid them. These are ways in which you may try to manage the sensory environment in order to better suit your sensory needs. These are things that you may already do without even noticing in order to help facilitate better regulation and maintain a calm, alert, attentive state. As you read through these lists, consider which of these activities most impact your regulation and attention—in a positive way or in a negative way. This will help you discover your pattern of sensory preferences. There may be entire sections that you feel do not impact your regulation or attention at all. There may be some activities that increase your arousal level or attention at one point in the day but decrease it at another point. For example, listening to loud rock music in the morning can help wake up your body and prepare for the day, but listening to the same music after a stressful day at work may send you "over the edge" and cause you to be more irritable; or going for a run in the morning can energize your body and help you be more alert, while going for a run after getting into an argument can help calm your body down. Here are some examples of adaptive activities, based on sensory preferences, that serve as a means to increase or decrease arousal level and attention throughout the day.

- *Tactile*
  - Twist your hair
  - Fidget with a toy
  - Move something around in your pocket with your hand
  - Pick at your cuticle or nails
  - Drum fingers or pencil on table
  - Rub your fingers on your lips
- *Visual*
  - Look out an open window
  - Turn off the lights

- Wear sunglasses
- Watch a fast-paced TV show
- Look at something spinning
- See people moving around you
- Sit in the front of the class
- Sit in the back of the class

- *Auditory*
  - Listen to classical music
  - Listen to hard rock
  - Hear a scratch on a chalkboard
  - Work with other people talking
  - Work in a quiet room
  - Sing or talk to self
  - Hear a clock ticking
  - Hear an air conditioner buzzing

- *Movement*
  - Rock your body slightly
  - Stand while working or eating
  - Sit or bounce on a yoga ball
  - Doodle while listening
  - Kick your legs back and forth while sitting
  - Push a chair back on two legs while sitting
  - Walk around while talking
  - Tap pencil or pen
  - Carry heavy objects

- *Taste*
  - Drink through a straw
  - Chew gum
  - Suck on hard candy

- Crunch on nuts, pretzels, or chips
- Crunch or suck on ice pieces
- Eat hot soup
- Chew on pencil/pen
- Bite on nails or cuticles
- Drink carbonated drink
- Suck, lick, bite on your lips or the inside of your cheeks

- *Smell*
  - Smell markers
  - Wear perfume, cologne, or scented lotion
  - Smell body odor
  - Smell garbage
  - Smell food cooking

Your sensory preferences as a teacher may also impact your students' regulation in a positive or negative way.[6] Does your preference for visual input—bright colors and fun designs—cause students to become easily distracted? Does your preference for low amounts of auditory input cause a deafening silence that actually makes it hard for students to focus? Do you get easily agitated when students crowd around you at circle time because the tactile input is too much, even though the students are using this as a means to connect with you?

It may also be helpful to reflect on how your sensory preferences have changed over the years. This is because the environment can influence our preferences. The changing of sensory preferences can be traced back to the neuroplasticity of the brain that we mentioned before. For example, children tend to have a much higher tolerance for spinning (a type of vestibular input) because they engage in more activities that stimulate that sensory system, such as rough and tumble play, rolling, hanging upside-down, and twirling. As we grow up and engage in fewer spinning-like activities, the connections in the brain change, resulting in more sensitivity to that type of input. Thinking back to your childhood, which sensory inputs do you recall being bothersome at home or at school? Do you still feel the same way about those bothersome sensory inputs or are you able to maintain better regulation now as an adult? In what way(s) have your sensory preferences changed since high school? Since college? What ways have you tailored your environment, both at home and in the classroom, to suit your sensory preferences? How might your current sensory preferences impact the regulation of your students, whether positively or negatively?

You can also use the list above to consider the sensory preferences of your students. We encourage you to have your students fill out a sensory preference questionnaire at the beginning of the year, available in Appendix C, to not only increase your awareness but also increase their awareness. Are there students who demonstrate more tactile sensory preferences by twirling their pencils, fidgeting with their sweatshirt strings, or holding an object in their hands? Are there students who demonstrate more vestibular sensory preferences by rocking back and forth during circle time, changing positions in their chair, or swinging every day at recess? Are there students who have more similar sensory preferences to you? Are there students who have sensory preferences that are dysregulating to you?

Let's be honest. You cannot meet the needs of all the different sensory preferences that exist in your classroom. But you can tailor the classroom environment to provide a wide variety of sensory experiences and adaptations that students can access when needed; the upcoming chapters will provide you with more ideas on how to do this. You can also refer back to the chart in Chapter 1 regarding sensory inputs that may be more calming and those that may be more stimulating. And you can use your knowledge of sensory preferences to understand why a student may, on a particular day, be having a difficult time engaging in classroom instruction or sitting at lunchtime or interacting with peers or attending to an assembly. Rather than interpreting a student's sensory preferences as annoying or distracting or unnecessary, reframe them as a form of regulation for the student and consider what you can do to keep yourself regulated when there is a mismatch between your sensory preferences and those of the student.

Defining Sensory Processing Disorder

As you've seen, each person has his own sensory preferences at any given time of day. While those preferences differ from person to person, there are some students (and adults) who do not respond to or organize sensory information in a functional way on a consistent basis. Rather than being viewed as simply a preference, this lack of functional response is considered to be a sensory processing disorder. **Sensory processing disorder (SPD)** *occurs when the nervous system cannot appropriately process sensory input, resulting in a maladaptive response that interferes with daily participation and functioning.*[6] Essentially, the brain has difficulty receiving and responding to sensory input, which then disrupts normal daily activities. The brain might respond too much to sensory input, resulting in a perceived sense of threat in a safe environment. Or the brain might respond too little to sensory input, resulting in the inability to respond to important information when needed.

SPD looks different for each person—adults and children alike. It may cause a fight, flight, or freeze response almost every time, sending out a signal of distress that communicates, "I can't do this!" or "This is too much!" or "I'm trying my hardest!"[6] It may cause confusion as to what the body is actually experiencing. It may cause frustration that the body won't do what the mind wants it to do. It may cause shame that others are constantly being disappointed. It may cause embarrassment that everyone else can do it. This is more than just a preference—it is a "can't" response rather than a "won't" response.[7] "Pushing through" is no longer an option (as with sensory preferences) because in this case the brain is neurologically not equipped to properly take in, process, or integrate the sensory input. There is a mismatch between the sensory input and the intended behavioral or motor output. In fact, this difference can actually be seen in the brain. Research shows that children with SPD, as compared to children without SPD, have differences in white matter connectivity which impacts the relaying of sensory information throughout the brain.[2,8]

It is worth reiterating that some students may internalize their sensory-based responses while others will externalize their responses. Look for students who not only pull away, scream, or express frustration but also for those who "check-out", stop talking, or express indifference. Typically, children will naturally select sensory-based activities that help them remain regulated. If a student chooses to hang upside-down on the monkey bars at recess, then they may be needing vestibular input to help them stay regulated. If a student is twirling their pencil in class then they may be needing tactile input to help them pay attention. These behaviors are helpful cues that we, as attuned teachers and adults in students' lives, can attend to and use to best support their regulation and learning.

However, children with SPD have a difficult time taking in and/or organizing sensory input in a way that is functional.[9] While they may be communicating

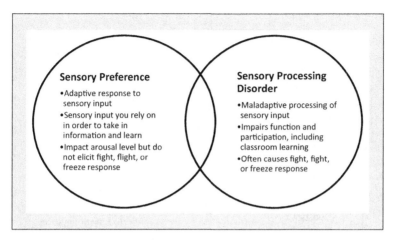

Sensory Preference
- Adaptive response to sensory input
- Sensory input you rely on in order to take in information and learn
- Impact arousal level but do not elicit fight, flight, or freeze response

Sensory Processing Disorder
- Maladaptive processing of sensory input
- Impairs function and participation, including classroom learning
- Often causes fight, fight, or freeze response

Figure 3.1 Sensory Preferences vs. Sensory Processing Disorder

Recognizing the difference between sensory preferences and sensory processing disorder (SPD) can help you identify the ways in which the sensory environment of the classroom impacts certain students, and to what degree those students may need support. Monitoring both sensory preferences and SPDs in your classroom will help your students to achieve "just right" nervous system arousal for improved attention and learning.

Taken from Chaves, J., & Taylor, A. (2020). *The "Why" Behind Classroom Behaviors: Integrative Strategies for Learning, Regulation, and Relationships.* Thousand Oaks, CA: Corwin.

the need for certain sensory inputs, such as spinning in a circle during class instruction, they need assistance with structuring the sensory activity to meet their sensory needs—this may include how long, how often, or how intense the activity is. Without this structure or support, children with SPD may actually become more dysregulated in their attempt to become regulated. Children with SPD may also need support in selecting activities that provide an ideal challenge to facilitate integration of all of their senses rather than leaning on the same activities over and over because they feel comfortable (and thus can avoid sensory inputs that are uncomfortable). This support is typically given in sensory integration therapy with a trained occupational therapist.

In Chapter 1 we identified the three main classifications for processing sensory information. These classifications are broken down even further when diagnosing SPD.[1,10] Again, this will assist you in better

45

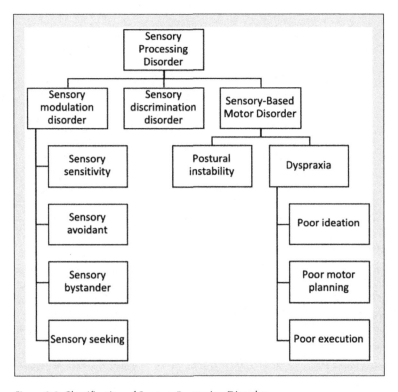

Figure 3.2 Classification of Sensory Processing Disorder

Sensory processing disorder (SPD) occurs when the nervous system cannot appropriately process sensory input, resulting in a maladaptive response that interferes with daily participation and functioning. The classification of SPD into distinct categories allows you to better identify the unique sensory needs of particular students in your classroom. However, it is not uncommon for students to demonstrate difficulty in multiple categories.

Adapted from Miller, L. J., Anzalone, M. E., Lane, S. J, Cermak, S. A, & Osten, E. T. (2007). Concept evolution in sensory integration: A proposed nosology for diagnosis. *American Journal of Occupational Therapy, 61*(2), 135–140.

identifying the unique sensory needs of your students, providing appropriate accommodations, and communicating your observations to professionals who can support those students even more. As a note, there is still differing consensus on the classification of SPD within the field of occupational therapy—more research is needed to clarify these categories.[11]

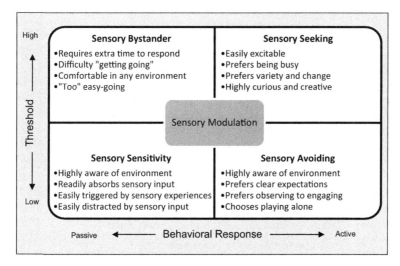

Figure 3.3 Categories of Sensory Modulation Disorder

Sensory modulation disorder can look different depending on the threshold of activation and behavioral response for the child. Sensory sensitivity and sensory avoiding are indications of overstimulation—the amount of sensory input is too much. Sensory bystander and sensory-seeking are indications of understimulation—the amount of sensory input is too little.

Adapted from Dunn, W. (1997). The impact of sensory processing abilities on the daily lives of young children and their families: A conceptual model. *Infant & Young Children*, 9(4), 23–35.

Sensory Modulation Disorder

Sensory modulation disorder can be divided into four categories: sensory sensitivity, sensory avoidant, sensory bystander, and sensory seeking[10]. Sensory sensitivity and sensory avoidant indicate a hyperresponsiveness or overstimulation to sensory input—a low threshold for the input. Sensory bystander and sensory seeking indicate a hyporesponsiveness or understimulation to sensory input—a high threshold for the input. Sensory sensitivity and sensory bystander are more passive responses to sensory input—a more indirect way of dealing with the input. Sensory avoidant and sensory seeking are more active responses to sensory input—a more direct way of dealing with the input.

- Sensory sensitivity
  - Highly aware of what is happening in the environment
  - Readily absorbs sensory input
  - Easily triggered by sensory experiences

- Sensory avoidant
  - Highly aware of what is happening in the environment
  - Prefers clear expectations and guidelines
  - Prefers observing rather than engaging
  - Chooses playing alone over playing with others

- Sensory bystander
  - Requires extra time to respond to sensory input
  - Difficulty "getting going" on a task
  - Comfortable in most any environment
  - Easy-going, almost to a fault

- Sensory seeking
  - Easily excitable
  - Prefers being busy, active, and engaged
  - Prefers variety and change
  - Highly curious and creative

Sensory modulation disorder can be complex; for our purposes we will talk in terms of overstimulation and understimulation for each sensory system. In both cases the brain has difficulty with inhibiting sensory input—either it happens too slowly or too quickly—resulting in too much sensory information or not enough sensory information. Sensory modulation disorders can be difficult to detect because symptoms are reflected in behavioral responses to the environment. Sometimes these behavioral responses may be overt, like covering ears and running away when a loud noise is heard; sometimes these behavioral responses may be covert, like staring around the room when a visually stimulating worksheet is too overwhelming. In both instances, the behavior of the student must be considered again as communication and, as a teacher, it is necessary to receive and interpret what is being communicated.

Children who are overstimulated (sensory sensitivity and sensory avoiding) in response to sensory input require less of a certain stimulus in order for their brains to detect that something has changed in their environment. They are "more sensitive, have a low threshold, and habituate slowly to sensory input."[6] Basically the level of sensory input is turned up too much. Students who have difficulty with sensory modulation may struggle with filtering out background noise such as the air conditioner or traffic outside the window. They may have to work harder to visually attend to a busy SMART board or social studies map. They may become easily excited when engaging in movement activities in PE class. Research shows that children who have an overstimulated response to sensory input more readily activate the "fight or flight" sympathetic nervous system, resulting in a heightened perception of sensory stimuli. At the same time, these children have decreased activation of the calming parasympathetic nervous system, causing a prolonged time to reach a state of regulation[12,13]. It is not uncommon for these children to have a co-diagnosis of anxiety and experience lower social competence.[14] As we discussed in Chapter 1, the brain remembers responses to sensory experiences, so the negative experience that the student may have while looking at a busy SMART board or hearing the air conditioner gets reinforced with each negative re-exposure, thus increasing the stress response and anticipatory stress response. For some children with SPD, this can result in toxic stress, impeding their ability to access higher brain areas required for social interaction, academic engagement, and learning.

Children who are understimulated (sensory seeking and sensory bystander) require more of a certain stimulus in order for their brains to detect that something has changed in their environment. They are "less sensitive, have a high threshold, and habituate quickly to sensory input."[6] Basically the level of sensory input is turned down too much. Students who are understimulated may need to fidget with an object in order to stay engaged and alert. They may move slowly and clumsily in PE class. They may constantly talk to themselves or make noises during quiet work time. They may seem like they're ignoring you. Much of the research in sensory modulation has been dedicated to sensory overstimulation, so there is still much to learn about the physiological responses of children who are understimulated. That being said, students who are sensory bystanders tend to be the most overlooked from a clinical standpoint because they are not disruptive and fly under the radar until they are older. Students who are sensory bystanders may have a co-diagnosis of depression because they are not experiencing pleasure in everyday activities due to their low registration of and passive response to sensory input.

Sensory Discrimination Disorder

Children with sensory discrimination disorder have difficulty telling the difference between sensory stimuli or using the information from stimuli in a functional manner. They may also have difficulty organizing sensory input or parsing out the fine details associated with certain sensations.[9,11] In other words, they can see the forest but not the trees. Students who have difficulty with sensory discrimination may dump out their entire backpack to look for an item because they cannot feel the difference between a pen and marker just by reaching inside. They may confuse the letters "b" and "d" or "p" and "q" when writing because they look the same. They may appear not to listen to instructions because when the teacher announces to "take out" a pencil they start to "talk about" a pencil. But the reality is that those subtle nuances are challenging for them. Each sensory system has a discriminatory function. Poor ability to discriminate can result in frustration and confusion when trying to interact with different sensory inputs; precision and efficiency are often compromised.[9] Oftentimes children with sensory modulation disorder also have sensory discrimination disorder because they are not appropriately interacting with the sensory input in a way that allows them to access higher level perception needed for discrimination.[15]

Sensory-Based Motor Disorder

Sensory-based motor disorder indicates a disconnect between the integration of sensory input and the intended motor output. This form of SPD can be further broken down into postural instability and dyspraxia. Postural instability results in difficulty with maintaining a stable upright position, particularly for extended periods of time and during movement activities. This may result in falling out of a chair, avoiding swings during recess, or leaning on peers during circle time. Dyspraxia, or difficulty with organizing motor actions, can be further broken down into difficulty with ideation, motor planning, and execution of movements.[15] Ideation is the ability to formulate an idea around what to do, motor planning is the ability to formulate a plan around how to do it, and execution is the ability to appropriately implement the plan. This may be reflected in a messy work station, poor coordination of scissors, avoidance of learning new games at recess, or frustration with handwriting. Integration of

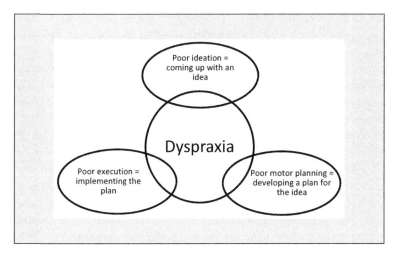

Figure 3.4 Forms of Dyspraxia

Dyspraxia, or difficulty with organizing motor actions, can be further broken down into difficulty with ideation, motor planning, and execution of movements. Ideation is the ability to formulate an idea around what to do, motor planning is the ability to formulate a plan around how to do it, and execution is the ability to appropriately implement the plan. All of these require high-level cognitive processes for organization, conceptualization, and creativity.

the tactile, proprioceptive, and vestibular systems is necessary for appropriate sensory-based motor processing in order to in order to achieve postural stability, perform various actions with our body, and manipulate other objects.[9] There is also a high degree of cognitive engagement that allows the student to generalize concepts, ideas, and plans to *novel* situations.[11] Students with postural instability and dyspraxia often have low self-esteem, self-confidence, and frustration tolerance around motor-based activities because they cannot trust that their bodies will do what their brains wants them to.[11,15] We will dive more into praxis and postural stability in Chapter 8.

Recognizing Different School-Based Sensory Needs

"It is important to recognize that children with SPD often try to impose more control in many areas of life because their bodies and the environment feel so out of control to them. This need for control and rigidity is their way of establishing a safe, predictable world that they can trust. Patience, understanding, and flexibility on your part, as a teacher, is therefore very important."[6] As mentioned in Chapter 2, a protective teacher–student relationship can positively impact the way in which a student responds to his sensory environment. For students with SPD, this effect is heightened when the sensory environment feels safe and predictable.

When you take a step back to assess the sensory environment at school, you can start to appreciate how stimulating a school day can be to students. You may even feel the impact of the stimulation yourself. The primary focus of this book is to delineate each of the eight sensory systems and highlight how they impact participation in school. This will help you better understand what might be underlying certain behaviors, recognize when a student may be experiencing a sensory processing disorder or may need extra sensory-based support in the classroom.

It is not uncommon for students with SPD to experience considerable stress throughout the school day. Students with SPD are working very hard to compensate for their difficulty integrating sensory input which impacts their "window of tolerance," or ability to handle or manage frustration.[6,16] Their brains and bodies must work harder to maintain a balance between the sympathetic and parasympathetic nervous systems. If a student's nervous system is already on edge due to having difficulty processing auditory input from the humming air conditioner and whispering of peers, for example, their ability to complete a frustrating math assignment will be even more limited. Additionally, as academic demands increase, dysregulation may also increase. The student may be able to curb some of this duress at times, but when additional stress is added to the nervous system this becomes increasingly challenging and sensory input becomes that much more dysregulating.[6] Thus, sensory-related behaviors can be exacerbated by stress, added demands, and life transitions, which may be why some children exhibit more sensory behaviors at school compared to home.[6]

Oftentimes there are early signs that indicate an SPD in infancy or toddlerhood, especially because there is a natural order of sensory integrative functioning; however some of these signs may be missed until the child reaches school.[9] Caregivers may not be aware of their child's SPD in infancy and toddlerhood so they may go unnoticed, or may be attributed to something else, such a fussy baby or a baby who had difficulty sleeping or eating or perhaps a baby who was less responsive. It is therefore helpful to know what types of questions to ask to get a better understanding of whether the behaviors we are seeing on the surface are potentially related to an underlying SPD.

Overlooking or mischaracterizing SPDs may continue to happen as children get older and enter school. As we've mentioned, it is important to reframe or shift our interpretation of behaviors as a form of communication. Remember, students are always communicating to us, either verbally or non-verbally, through how they behave. This is true for SPD as well.

Non-verbal cues *include anything a student is communicating with their body position, facial expression, posture, and gestures.* Some of the distress signs below are examples of non-verbal cues. Not only is it important to monitor the non-verbal cues from your students, but also within yourself. Attending to non-verbal cues in yourself and in your students can help to decrease the threat responses in your students as you learn to co-regulate with them quickly and effectively.[6] This will also provide you with valuable information about how to best support the students you work with. This knowledge helps us better know how to navigate challenging emotional moments and de-escalate students who are experiencing threat responses. Attunement to students' non-verbal cues will help you to better understand what each student is attempting to communicate. As noted, there are certain non-verbal signs that will likely be communicated by students who are struggling to modulate sensory input.

One way to help shift our interpretation and reframe certain behaviors is to identify them as "distress signs," especially when it seems as though a student is exhibiting disruptive, manipulative, or inappropriate behaviors. It is important to slow down, look a little deeper, and take a moment to understand what distress sign the student is communicating to us through their behaviors. Often times sensory-related dysregulation results in physiological changes—changes to the body and its functions. The internal changes that the student experiences are generally reflected in behaviors that can be seen by other people, like yourself. Recognizing these distress signs is a critical part of helping a student get back to a regulated state in order to facilitate improved engagement and learning. As mentioned, many of these distress signs can be misinterpreted as behaviors that are disruptive or manipulative on the surface, when in fact they are signs of an SPD. Some distress signs indicate sensory overload, some indicate the need for more sensory input, and others can indicate both. *All* of these signals indicate that you need to take a break from the activity, find a calm place for the student, and help the student attain a regulated state before moving forward.[11] Thus, co-regulation between you and the student must occur. This is not an exhaustive list, but here are some common signs of sensory-related distress:

- Hands over ears
- Tuning out
- Refusal to leave a caregiver
- Irritability
- Avoidance of social interactions
- Rigidity
- Uncontrollable meltdowns
- Sweating
- Heavy breathing
- Wide eyes
- Disorganization of behavior and thoughts
- Aggressive behaviors
- Poor frustration tolerance
- Physical withdrawal
- Excessive talking
- Repeated yawning
- Excessive fidgeting or moving around too much
- Rolling around on the floor during circle time
- Getting too close to others
- Difficulty transitioning from one task to the next
- Fleeting attention

"Students who are more susceptible to changes in sensory input, due to difficulty with modulation, typically respond by changing their *attention, affect, or arousal* level."[6] Because these three areas often influence each other they can be tricky to tease apart.

- Change in *attention* includes how engaged or disengaged the student appears.[6] If a student is "checking out" it could signify that the student is experiencing too much stimulation and needing to escape or that the student is needing more stimulation in order to adequately participate. "Checking out" may look like a student staring off into space, looking drowsy, gazing out the window. If a student appears hyperattentive it is likely they are on high alert because of feeling overstimulated. Hyperattentive students may have wide eyes, their eyes may be darting around the room, they may react to every little noise, and they may appear tense.

- Change in *affect* includes the emotional expressions of a student.[6] If a student goes quickly from laughing and smiling to being quiet and serious, it could be a sign the student is experiencing too much stimulation and feels threatened. If a student appears sad or bored despite the majority of the class demonstrating uplifting and interactive behaviors, it could indicate the student requires more stimulation in order to engage in learning.

- Change in *arousal* level includes how alert a student appears based on behavior.[6] If a student is running away, screaming aloud, or getting overly excited about something, it is a strong indication that there is too much sensory input. If a student is acting sluggish, is slow to initiate an activity, or hiding off in a corner, it may be a sign they are overstimulated and shutting down or that they require more sensory input to fully engage in the experience.

One thing worth mentioning here is that logic cannot mitigate the felt experience of a student with SPD.[11] No matter how "silly" it may seem that a student is responding a certain way in a certain situation, that experience is real to the student. For example, a student might demand that the straps of their backpack are so loose that their backpack nearly drags on the floor and slaps against their ankles with each step. But that particular setting is the only way that they can tolerate the tactile input from the backpack on their body. Logically, you could try to convince them that carrying a backpack higher up takes less stress off the shoulders and would make it easier to walk. Yet, you cannot talk the student out of how they feel when the backpack is in a typical position, no matter how much care or co-regulation you offer while doing so. The student must be able to internalize their own sense of safety first in order to feel intrinsic control over the situation and experience emotional security.[11] A student with SPD needs to know that they will be heard, and that they can be in control of their own space and body.

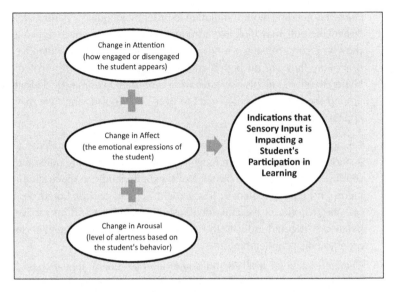

Figure 3.5 Monitoring Non-Verbal Cues

One way that you can recognize the sensory responses in your students is to pay attention to their non-verbal cues. These are anything a student is communicating with their body position, facial expression, posture, and gestures. Three ways in which you may see changes in a student's non-verbal cues in response to sensory input include attention, affect, and arousal.

Additional Supports for Students with Sensory Needs

While it is important for teachers to have foundational knowledge in sensory processing, its impact on regulation, distress signs to look out for, and ways to integrate sensory activities in the classroom for a wide range of student needs, there are certain circumstances where a student will require more than what a teacher can provide. Occupational therapists are often on the educational support team and have specialized knowledge in sensory processing, among other things like fine motor skills, handwriting, feeding, and cognitive functioning.[17] *Intervention from an occupational therapist is warranted when sensory needs interfere with a student's ability to function and participate in school-based activities.* They can provide additional resources for teachers, make suggestions for specific accommodations a student may require, be involved in the Individualized Education Plan (IEP) process, and work individually with students who have considerable sensory-based needs.

When is it appropriate to consult with an occupational therapist regarding a student's sensory needs? First and foremost, consider the impact of the sensory need on the student's participation in learning, functioning in the school environment, and ability to engage in meaningful activities. Talk about your concerns with other teachers, including specialty teachers who may have a unique lens when it comes to interacting with the student. Bear in mind the impact of your concerns on future participation and function in school—how might what you're seeing impact skill development and ability to meet demands down the line? Using the information in the following chapters, gather concrete evidence and examples that highlight patterns of sensory-based behavior occurring.

Keep an open mind when you have a student who is exhibiting unusual, atypical, or disruptive behaviors. Is a student who is talking too much, bouncing around the room, and getting into fights with peers at recess actually experiencing a sensory processing disorder? Rather than having that student be identified as a problem child with behavioral problems, they may actually have an SPD. There is often much more underlying the behavior of our students; SPD can often be missed or misunderstood. Talk with a trusted occupational therapy colleague about what you are seeing and in what ways the sensory environment might be triggering maladaptive behaviors or resulting in poor participation in that particular student.

Introducing the need for occupational therapy services is usually a delicate dance with caregivers. There is no magic formula for recommending therapy or for knowing what may happen if therapy is not pursued. Some caregivers will err on the side of caution while others will want to wait and see what happens down the line. Research suggests that without intervention, 50% of children found to be sensitive to sensory input at 2 years old retained that sensitivity at 4–5 years old.[18,19] What's important to remember is that neuroplasticity typically happens more quickly and more dramatically with early intervention—particularly before the age of 7 or 8 years old. This is not to say that neuroplasticity cannot happen after that age; it just may take longer and require more intentional effort.[9] Your early recognition of potential sensory processing differences, and subsequent action to speak with the school's occupational therapist to determine the next steps, will make a world of difference.

Your primary role when meeting with caregivers is to present your tangible concerns, provide them with resources available at the school, and highlight what is already being done to support the student.[6] It is important not to jump to conclusions or name any particular diagnoses without proper assessment. All of this must be done within the context of relationship. Your regulation will set the tone for the meeting, so try to remain calm and establish a safe, trust-filled environment. Be willing to listen and learn from the caregivers. Be open to cultural considerations that may be a factor. Be able to delineate the strengths of the student and the strengths of the caregivers.[6] Identify and describe stories of resilience and hope that you see in the student. Be receptive to alternative solutions that will allow the student to thrive. Be aware that the student's behaviors may look different at home than they do at school.

Some helpful questions to answer when considering the sensory needs of a student include:[6]

- When do you see the behavior?
- How often do you see the behavior?
- For how long does the behavior last?
- Does the behavior happen in other environments or classes?
- When did the behavior start?
- Has the behavior happened in the past?
- Are there patterns associated with this behavior?

Recall that stress can mediate how we process sensory input, so, for some students, days that are particularly demanding or challenging may result in more difficulty managing sensory input.[6] This is true for all of us, to a degree. When the responses to sensory inputs start to consistently impact how a student engages at school or carries out daily routines, that is a sign that more support is necessary. As teachers you can help to lessen the stress and dysregulation that students experience in response to sensory inputs by making alterations to your classroom setup and providing access to certain accommodations. The upcoming chapters will explore each sensory system in depth to help you recognize more specific distress signals and identify which sensory input may be changing a student's attention, affect, or arousal, as well as specific school-based strategies that you can use to build a sensory-smart classroom. These strategies can be used to accommodate students' sensory preferences, as well as students with specific SPDs.

References

1. Miller, L. J., Anzalone, M. E., Lane, S. J, Cermak, S. A, & Osten, E. T. (2007). Concept evolution in sensory integration: a proposed nosology for diagnosis. *American Journal of Occupational Therapy, 61*(2), 135–140.

2. Chang, Y. S., Owen, J. P., Desai, S. S., Hill, S. S., Arnett, A. B., Harris, J., & Mukherjee, P. (2014). Autism and sensory processing disorders: Shared white matter disruption in sensory pathways but divergent connectivity in social-emotional pathways. *PloS One, 9*(7), e103038.

3. The Centers for Disease Control and Prevention (April 5, 2019). Data and statistics on Autism Spectrum Disorder. Retrieved from https://www.cdc.gov/ncbddd/autism/data.html (Accessed August 2020).

4. Ahn, R. R., Miller, L. J., Milberger, S., & McIntosh, D. N. (2004). Prevalence of parents' perceptions of sensory processing disorders among kindergarten children. *American Journal of Occupational Therapy, 58*(3), 287–293.

5. Cronin, A. (2003). *Asynchronous Development and Sensory Integration Intervention in the Gifted and Talented Population.* Reno, NV: Davidson Institute for Talent Development. http://www.davidsongifted.org/search-database/entry/a10251

6. Chaves, J. & Taylor, A. (2020). *The "Why" Behind Classroom Behaviors: Integrated Strategies for Learning, Regulation, and Relationships.* Thousand Oaks, CA: Corwin.

7. Siegel, D. J., & Bryson, T. P. (2016). *No-Drama Discipline: The Whole-Brain Way to Calm the Chaos and Nurture Your Child's Developing Mind.* New York: Bantam.

8. Owen, J. P., Marco, E. J., Desai, S., Fourie, E., Harris, J., Hill, S. S., ... & Mukherjee, P. (2013). Abnormal white matter microstructure in children with sensory processing disorders. *Neuroimage: Clinical, 2*, 844–853.

9. Ayers, A. J. (2005). *Sensory Integration and the Child: Understanding Hidden Sensory Challenges.* Los Angeles, CA: Western Psychological Services.

10. Dunn, W. (1997). The impact of sensory processing abilities on the daily lives of young children and their families: A conceptual model. *Infant & Young Children, 9*(4), 23–35.

11. Burpee, J. (2015). *Sensory Integrative Intensive Continuing Education Course.* Medfield, MA: Education Resources, Inc.

12. Schaaf, R. C., Benevides, T. W., Blanche, E., Brett-Green, B. A., Burke, J., Cohn, E., ... & Schoen, S. A. (2010) Parasympathetic functions in children with sensory processing disorder. *Frontiers in Integrative Neuroscience, 4*, 4.

13. Schoen, S. A., Miller, L. J., Brett-Green, B. A., & Nielsen, D. M. (2009). Physiological and behavioral differences in sensory processing: A comparison of children with Autism Spectrum Disorder and sensory modulation disorder. *Frontiers in Integrative Neuroscience, 3*, 3.

14. Ben-Sasson, A., Carter, A. S., & Briggs-Gowan, M. J. (2009). Sensory over-responsivity in elementary school: prevalence and social-emotional correlates. *Journal of Abnormal Child Psychology, 37*(5), 705–716. https://doi.org/10.1007/s10802-008-9295-8

15. Case-Smith, J., Allen, A. S., & Pratt, P. N. (2001). *Occupational Therapy for Children* (6th ed.). St. Louis, MO: Mosby.

16. Siegel, D. J. (1999). *The Developing Mind: Toward a Neurobiology of Interpersonal Experience.* New York: Guilford Press.

17. American Occupational Therapy Association (2016). Occupational therapy in school settings. https://www.aota.org/About-Occupational-Therapy/Professionals/CY/school-settings.aspx#:~:text=They%20support%20a%20student's%20ability,positive%20behaviors%20necessary%20for%20learning. (Accessed August 2020).

18. Goldsmith, H. H., Lemery-Chalfant, K., Schmidt, N. L., Arnerson, C. L., & Schmidt, C. K. (2007). Longitudinal analyses of affect, temperament, and childhood psychopathology. *Twin Research and Human Genetics, 10*(1), 118–126.

19. Goldsmith, H. H., Van Hulle, C. A., Arnerson, C. L., Schreiber, J. E., & Gernsbacher, M. A. (2006). A population-based twin study of parentally reported tactile and auditory defensiveness in young children. *Journal of Abnormal Child Psychology, 34*(3), 393–407.

The Visual System

Javier complained of headaches almost every day at school. Mr. Albright, his math teacher, often saw him rubbing his eyes or looking around the room when doing math worksheets. Mr. Albright found himself becoming increasingly frustrated as he often needed to remind Javier to focus and keep working after he completed only a few equations. Not to mention Javier was falling behind his peers in his work. When Mr. Albright approached Javier about his observations, Javier commented, "I don't know. It's just hard to stay focused. There are just so many numbers on the paper."

As the school year progressed Javier continued to struggle with staying on task in math class, and even had a few outbursts where he threw his paper on the floor and yelled, "This is too hard!" This was confusing to Mr. Albright because Javier could easily solve the equations in his head when asked by Mr. Albright. It didn't seem like the math itself was hard to Javier.

His parents reported to Mr. Albright that Javier often came home from school exhausted and required extra effort to complete his homework despite grasping the concepts. Maybe he was struggling with his attention overall? Javier also recently started to decline doing art projects at home because they created more frustration for him. In the past Javier loved creating things with markers and glue and scissors. Maybe he was just growing out of this interest?

It is easy to assume the visual system is processing information correctly when a student isn't overtly complaining about blurred vision or not being able to see something. They may not actually know any different because that is how they have always seen the world. Because vision plays a major role in our everyday life, and particularly in the classroom, this sensory system should be prioritized when considering why a student may be struggling.

What is the Visual System?

Visual input *is what we see.* In school this may be "lights in the gymnasium, colors in art class, facial expressions of peers, recognizing letters, orienting numbers correctly, copying shapes, completing worksheets, and following the teacher at the front of the classroom."[1] School provides a huge amount of visual input throughout the day.

As seen in the diagram, visual input is received by the eye and then processed by the occipital lobe. Just like any other sensory input, certain visual information can be calming and regulating to our nervous system while other visual input may be alerting or overstimulating. Fast-moving, bright, and colorful videos, like GoNoodle®, may be visually overwhelming to some students. Some research even finds that fast-paced cartoons can be detrimental to a child's ability to focus and attend.[2] Additionally, busy visual fields or crowded worksheets may also be a source of stress for students because their brain may have difficulty with processing large amounts of visual input at one time. Some students will become frustrated and exasperatedly fall on the floor when presented with a page full of math

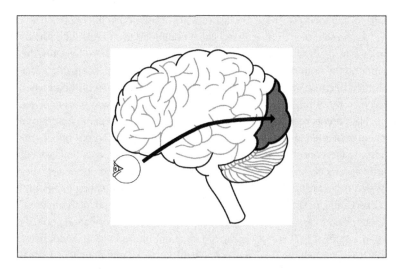

Figure 4.1 The Visual System

Sensory input for the visual system is received by the eye and then transmitted to the visual cortex in the occipital lobe for processing.

problems, for example. If you decrease the visual field and provide them with one math problem at a time, they may experience more success in managing their frustration and completing the work.

Another example of a how visual input can be overwhelming to students is lighting. It can be helpful to take a moment and think about the lighting in your classroom, in the hallways of your school, and in larger auditoriums or cafeterias. Research shows that fluorescent lightening is actually overwhelming to some students and even negatively impacts their attention and learning, particularly students diagnosed with ADHD, ASD, and SPD.[3] Conversely, natural lighting from the sun can actually have a healing, restorative impact on the brain.[4]

Visual input from the walls can also influence regulation. Pastel colors tend to be more regulating and calming, while bright colors tend to be more stimulating and alerting. Research has shown that students are actually able to learn more efficiently when there is less visual input on the walls.[5] Consider limiting the amount of artwork and posters in your classroom and only include information that facilitates participation in learning. Because the brain readily responds to novel sensory input, bear in mind that changing the visual input on the walls may lead most students to attend to that input for a period of time; this can work in your favor or against you.

If you notice a student who complains of headaches, such as Javier, or you see them blinking rapidly, this may be a sign that they are overwhelmed by the visual input presented to them. Other signs of difficulty with processing visual input include shielding the eyes, squinting, bending over something to look more closely, avoiding eye contact, or having difficulty focusing. Alternatively, when a student is not receiving enough visual input, this can result in boredom, feeling tired, or losing place when looking at something.[1] It important to find a balance in providing visual stimulation in a classroom to keep students regulated and engaged.

The visual system can be broken down into two different types of vision, central vision and peripheral vision, which are both used in order to see things in our environment. **Central vision** *helps us to see what is directly in front of us and attend to more intricate details; it works like a tunnel to allow us to focus.* **Peripheral vision** *helps us to see outside of the tunnel of the central vision of our eyes, like something approaching from behind or from the right or left.* Movement is something that primarily stimulates our peripheral vision, which makes peripheral vision important for our sense of safety. For example, if a student does not see a peer approaching from the right and the peer just appears in front of the student, it may be startling to the student. Our spatial awareness and ability to navigate the environment is highly dependent on peripheral vision.

The **vestibulo-ocular reflex (VOR)** *is an interaction between the vestibular and visual system that allows our eyes to stay stable when our head moves or for our head to stay stable when our eyes move.* The communication between these two systems is integral for our balance and ability to stay in an upright seated position when doing activities like reading and writing. The VOR also helps with eye-hand coordination activities, such as tying a shoe, catching a ball, cutting with scissors, and stringing beads.

The visual system often works in conjunction with the auditory and language systems to help with reading, writing, and math.[1] Social engagement with others also relies heavily on the vision information we receive from non-verbal cues, such as facial expressions, body posture, and hand gestures. We use visual input from reading lips in order to complement auditory information when talking with others.[6] Think about a time you were in a loud place, like a crowded restaurant, and how much more you focused on the lips of the person talking to you in order to fully understand them.

Visual perception is different from our eyes actually being able to see. It is not uncommon for students to have 20/20 vision yet struggle with visual perception. **Visual perception** *is a set of "higher level cognitive skills for how we utilize the visual input received by the brain."*[1] It is what we do with and how we interpret the visual input we take in. Visual perception includes how we are able to focus on and attend to visual input (visual attention); remember, encode, and recall information that we see (visual memory); make sense of different shapes and objects (visual form); and utilize visual information in space (visual-spatial skills).[1] Students are using their visual perceptual skills, for example, when they are drawing or copying information from the board, searching for items in their backpack, remaining focused when engaging in a highly visual task such as reading or writing, and writing within the lines of their notebooks.

Oculo-motor skills, on the other hand, *refer to how the muscles of the eyes are working to allow the eyes to see.* This includes how well the eye can see near and far (acuity), how the eyes work together (convergence), how they are able to follow an object (tracking), and if they move back and forth rapidly in certain situations (saccadic movements).[1] Oculo-motor deficits are typically screened for by a pediatrician that may result in a referral to an ophthalmologist or developmental optometrist. A difficulty in any of these

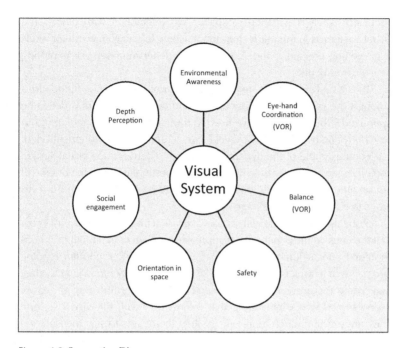

Figure 4.2 Supportive Diagram

The visual system plays a critical role in how a child interacts with and understands their environment. The diagram below outlines the primary ways in which the visual system impacts us on a regular basis.

areas is more likely a result of how the eye itself is working (or not working) and not a result of how the brain is processing what the eye sees. In other words, this is not an indication of sensory processing issues related to vision. That said, it is not uncommon for children (and adults) to struggle with any combination of visual processing, visual perception, and oculo-motor skills.

How does the Visual System Impact Regulation and Learning?

We rely the most on the visual system to gain an understanding about our environment. In fact, research suggests that the processing and storage of visual information requires more space in the brain than the combination of all other sensory systems.[7] It provides a large amount of information about our safety, navigation in space, and interaction with others. The visual system is particularly important when learning new motor skills (e.g., getting dressed, tying shoes, forming letters/numbers) or exploring new environments.

The visual system is reliant upon strong integrative foundations amongst the vestibular, proprioceptive, and tactile systems in order to be optimized.[8] This means that we need to have a good understanding of our own body and how our body moves in space. The VOR, as aforementioned, is a good example of the dynamic relationship between the visual system and other sensory systems. Without a strong vestibular sense, the brain will not be able to successfully hold the head and neck stable while our eyes move to read what is on a page in a book.

Students who struggle with processing visual information may not know that the lines on the paper are not supposed to move or that math problems shouldn't appear jumbled on the page or that feeling tired after reading two pages in a book is not typical. Like Javier in the opening vignette, they may know the answer and understand the concepts but they get easily overwhelmed when integrating that information with the visual system. They are exerting much more energy than their peers to stay focused and follow along. Oftentimes visual processing differences can be an indication of another learning difference as well, such as non-verbal learning disorder, ADHD, or ASD.[8]

Here are several examples of common classroom activities that require a high level of visual processing:

- *Reading*

  Discerning the difference between letters and numbers, scanning across a page, and remaining attentive to the task all require the visual system to function properly. This requires not only appropriate sensory-related visual processing but also more complex visual perceptual skills. The visual system helps to filter out information that is not important to the task of reading, such as a light flickering, a peer moving in their seat, a teacher writing on the board, or a pencil case on the desk, to allow the brain to process the information.

- *Writing*

  Similar to reading, writing requires the ability to differentiate letters and numbers, move your eyes across the page, and remain attentive.

Additionally, writing requires the ability to orient to the margins and the line, maintain appropriate sizing, and space letters, words, and numbers appropriately. Our visual perceptual skills—what we do with the information we see—are critical to the development of legible writing. You may notice that as students progress in their writing skills, the motor aspect of writing becomes more automatic, which allows for less reliance on the visual system (you can probably write a sentence fairly accurately between the lines on paper without looking because of many years of practice!).

Copying from the board is a very common classroom writing activity that utilizes many parts of our visual system. A student must filter out information on the board that is not relevant, focus on the words that need to be copied, shift the eyes back to the paper to write, and then complete this cycle again until the task is completed.

- *Engaging with peers*

  It may not seem like it, but the visual system is important during social interactions. When interacting with peers, a student relies on the visual system to practice attuned listening. This means that the student relies on their visual system to understand and interpret more subtle non-verbal social cues, and gather more information based on visual cues like facial expression and body posture, to better understand what is being conveyed verbally. Unconsciously, students read the lips of others when they are interacting with them, particularly in loud or stimulating environments like in the cafeteria or at recess, in order to "fill in" what is being said verbally—again, a practice that relies on visual processing.

- *Navigating the environment*

  Classrooms are busy places with a lot of furniture and activity. In order to safely navigate the environment, without bumping into people or objects, a student must use the visual system. This is true when getting up to sharpen a pencil, carry a tray through the cafeteria, climb the playground equipment, and put an instrument back in its case. As a student learns the environment they will begin to integrate the visual input with motor memory and not need to rely as much on the visual system, until something novel pops up in the classroom—such as the desks being rearranged in a different pattern.

- *Participating in physical education*

    Due to the large number of balance-related and eye-hand coordination-related activities involved in physical education, the VOR plays a critical role. For example, maintaining a stable visual field when running so you don't feel like everything is bouncing up and down constantly, or following a ball through the air and then moving towards a ball to catch it without losing balance or losing track of the ball. Navigating the environment is also important in PE and relies on visual processing.

We know that it may be difficult to determine, during the course of a busy day in a busy classroom, whether a student is overstimulated or understimulated with visual sensory input, or is having a difficult time discriminating sensory information. However, we want to provide you with some signs to look out for and behaviors to consider. The important thing is that you are being curious about why a student may be demonstrating different behaviors or presenting with challenges in their learning. If you have more questions you can certainly reach out to the occupational therapist on staff at your school.

Here we expand upon signs taken from our book *The "Why" Behind Classroom Behaviors: Integrative Strategies for Learning, Regulation, and Relationships,* in order to help you determine if there is a pattern of challenges that may indicate a sensory processing disorder.

When a student's visual system is *understimulated* you may see the following:

- Engages in visual posturing, such as putting fingers in front of face
- Complains eyes are tired when looking at a book
- Poor attention to detail; tends to only see the big picture
- Difficulty focusing on a still image; prefers fast-moving images
- Frequently looks around the room
- Likes bright colors, such as always needing to highlight material or use colored pens
- Twirls pens or pencils in front of face
- Has difficulty getting from one place to another; gets lost easily
- Needs help finding objects that seem readily apparent
- Doesn't notice when someone enters or leaves the room

Experience It!—Visual Overstimulation

Sit down at your computer and find an interesting, cognitively engaging article to read online. Enable pop-ups on your browser while you are reading the article.

Reflect on the following questions afterwards:

1) How much longer did it take to read the article with the pop-ups turned on?

2) What did you have to concentrate on more/less while reading the article?

3) How long did it take for you to re-engage with the article after each time a pop-up appeared?

This scenario is designed to help you better understand what a student with overstimulation to visual input might experience on a regular basis. They get easily distracted and overwhelmed with other visual input that is in the environment, such as posters on the walls or extra writing on the board. It is challenging to filter out that input and they must constantly try to re-engage with the task at-hand, which can become taxing after a while.

When a student's visual system is *overstimulated* you may see the following:

- Avoids being in a room with bright lights
- Squints or rubs eyes when coming in from recess
- Covers one eye when looking at something
- Avoids eye contact; looks off to the side when speaking
- Difficulty focusing on a crowded picture
- Skips math problems
- Skips lines when reading
- Complains of headaches or fatigue when reading, writing, or copying from the board

- Gets overwhelmed in crowded places with a lot of people moving around, such as PE, the cafeteria, or recess
- Becomes flustered with word searches, crossword puzzles, and mazes
- Easily distracted by people moving around the room

When a student's visual system cannot *discriminate* you may see the following:

- Has difficulty finding a specified object in a busy/complex picture
- Difficulty copying from the board
- Difficulty replicating an image, such as a map or clock or shape
- Poor ability to categorize or sort
- Confuses similar looking shapes, numbers, and letters (e.g., +/x, 6/9, b/d)
- Poor sizing, spacing, or placement on the line when writing
- Attends to parts of assignments but misses the whole picture
- Struggles with cutting along the lines
- Trips over objects when navigating the school environment

Note: Lack of visual discrimination often indicates a visual processing difference that may need to be evaluated by a developmental optometrist.

Sensory-Smart Visual Strategies for Every Classroom

Note: The first two paragraphs in this section will be reiterated in each chapter in order to ensure clarity and consistency. The principles will be applied to the opening vignette that differs in each chapter.

After determining a particular student's response to visual input, it's important to have some strategies in your back pocket to help support those needs. As teachers, we know you have so much to consider and so many students to support. Remember that you can always reach out to the school occupational therapist for more help; these strategies are not meant to replace additional therapy. However, implementing some of these strategies can help the overall regulation and learning of the majority of students in your class.

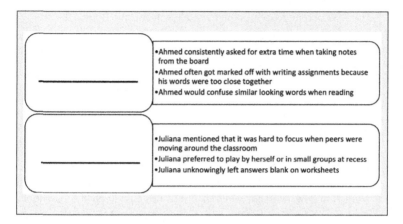

Figure 4.3 Interactive Scenario

Read the stories about students below that describe *patterns* the teacher has observed over several months. Determine if the student is experiencing difficulty with visual understimulation, overstimulation, or discrimination.

Through attending to your nonverbal cues, monitoring your tone of voice, and maintaining a calm presence with your students you will send them a message of safety and comfort while also supporting their sensory needs.[1] In the opening vignette Mr. Albright might tell Javier, "I understand that you are getting frustrated with your math problems. Maybe it would help to cover up the other problems on the page so you don't get overwhelmed?"

Just like anything new, progress takes time; making new neural connections takes time. Give each strategy a few weeks to see how your students respond and adapt to the changes you make, then reassess what may need to be adjusted. There may be a combination of strategies that a student may need, which often requires a trial and error process.[1] Try not to get discouraged if only small changes are seen; these are important neurological stepping stones towards a larger goal. For example, Mr. Albright might initially have Javier block out all the remaining math problems on the paper, then move to folding the paper in quarters, then move to folding the paper in half. This allows for scaffolded support that brings a "just right" challenge to Javier by setting him up for success without flooding his nervous system. Remember that if a student has a strong emotional reaction to completing a certain academic task, this means they need some type of scaffolding—or instructional techniques that support their learning process.

Here we expand upon strategies taken from our book *The "Why" Behind Classroom Behaviors: Integrative Strategies for Learning, Regulation, and Relationships,* in order to support students with their visual processing.

To promote appropriate visual processing *for all students:*

- Use natural sunlight as much as possible. When sunlight is not available then try to use ambient light from lamps rather than using the overhead fluorescent lighting
- Remove unnecessary visual input from the classroom walls, including: old artwork, posters not relevant to current lesson plans, items hanging from the ceiling, bright designs. Keep the essentials such as: a clock, daily schedule, homework agenda, posters relevant to the current lesson plan, and signs that serve as directives
- Make a visual schedule for the day using pictures. The visual schedule should represent each activity, and be split up into a morning and afternoon schedule
- Balance the amount and type of colors used in the room. Pastel colors are generally more calming than bold, bright colors
- Limit the frequency at which you change visual information hanging on the walls, such as posters and artwork
- Use a visual timer, such as one with a red indicator, to help students visualize the amount of time remaining for certain tasks
- Consider the colors and prints of the clothing you wear
- Position your body near the visual input you are referencing, such as a diagram or writing on the board, or use a pointer stick to do the same
- Get approval to paint your classroom a warm, calming color

To provide *more* visual input for *understimulation:*

- Use paper with red and blue lines to provide contrast to help with placement on the line
- Print worksheets on colored paper with high contrast
- Highlight important areas on worksheets to facilitate attention
- Have the student use different colors of pencils when writing

- Face the desk towards a window
- Encourage the student to sit in the front of the classroom
- Use videos to reinforce what was taught by the teacher
- Encourage the student to use a brightly colored guide when reading

To provide *less* visual input for *overstimulation:*

- Use reading and writing corrals during independent work. Binders and heavy-duty folders are good economical ways to create quick and temporary visual barriers
- Fold worksheets into quarters and have the child complete one quarter at a time to prevent overstimulation
- Decrease the number of math problems on the page
- Use a finger as a guide to follow along when reading
- Make a rectangular frame on a bookmark as a guide to follow along when reading
- Increase the font size on worksheets and reading materials
- Allow the student to wear sunglasses in the classroom
- Allow the student to sit in the front of the classroom
- Encourage the student to take "eye breaks" by looking around the room for several seconds before refocusing on their work
- Encourage the student to take "eye breaks" by closing their eyes for several seconds before refocusing on their work

To help support difficulty with *discrimination:*

- Highlight important areas on worksheets to facilitate attention
- Make a number and letter "quick-reference sheet" for the desk with commonly forgotten or reversed symbols
- Use a slantboard or 3-inch binder to promote better visual attention and convergence
- Remove extraneous information from around the dry erase board or assignment board

- Make the font size larger on worksheets
- Use paper with individual boxes for each letter, three-lined paper, or extra-wide ruled paper
- Encourage the student to practice mazes and dot-to-dots
- Encourage the student to verbally describe what they see

Note: Lack of visual discrimination often indicates a visual processing difference that may need to be evaluated by a developmental optometrist.

Special Accommodations in Writing and Reading to Consider for Children with Visual-based Challenges

- Make font sizes larger and use larger width paper
- Use a consistent font without tails or serifs
- Increase spacing between words and use double-spacing between lines for easier readability
- Use three-lined paper, extra-wide ruled paper, or paper with individual boxes
- Use verbal mnemonics to help with remembering the letter/number strokes
- Use proprioceptive input, like tracing the letters or forming the letters in the air, to help with remembering letter/number strokes
- Use tactile input, like forming letters in sand or shaving cream, to help with remembering the letter/number strokes
- Use reading guides to help the eyes focus on relevant material

Reflective Activity

Now that you know more about the visual system and its impact on learning and regulation, think about how you can apply this information to your classroom.

Ways I already support the visual systems of my students	• •
New ways that I can support the visual systems of my students	• •
Students who may need additional visual-based support	• •
Ways I notice that I process visual input	• •

References

1. Chaves, J., & Taylor, A. (2020). *The "Why" behind Classroom Behaviors: Integrated Strategies for Learning, Regulation, and Relationships.* Thousand Oaks, CA: Corwin.

2. Christakis, D. A. (2011). The effects of fast-paced cartoons. *Pediatrics, 128*(4), 772–774.

3. Kinnealey, M., Pfeiffer, B., Miller, J., Roan, C., Shoener, R., & Ellner, M. L. (2012). Effect of classroom modification on attention and engagement of students with autism or dyspraxia. *American Journal of Occupational Therapy, 66,* 511–519.

4. Doidge, N. (2016). *The Brain's Way of Healing: Remarkable Discoveries and Recoveries from the Frontiers of Neuroplasticity.* New York: Penguin Books.

5. Fisher, A. V., Godwin, K. E., & Seltman, H. (2014). Visual environment, attention allocation, and learning in young children: When too much of a good thing may be bad. *Psychological Science, 25*(7), 1362–1370.

6. Rosenblum, L. (2011). *See What I'm Saying: The Extraordinary Powers of Our Five Senses.* New York: W. W. Norton & Co.

7. Sherman, C. (August 12, 2019). The senses: Vision. Retrieved from https://www.dana.org/article/the-senses-vision/ (Accessed August 2020).

8. Ayers, A. J. (2005). *Sensory Integration and the Child: Understanding Hidden Sensory Challenges*. Los Angeles, CA: Western Psychological Services.

9. Kibby, M. Y., Dyer, S. M., Vadnais, S. A., Jagger, A. C., Casher, G. A., & Stacy, M. (2015). Visual processing in reading disorders and attention-deficit/hyperactivity disorder and its contribution to basic reading ability. *Frontiers in Psychology, 6*, 1635.

5 The Auditory System

Liliana was a smart, engaged student who had a knack for science class. She was curious and asked great questions during large-group instruction. But when it came time for semi-structured group work, Liliana seemed to shut down—she didn't give any input to the group, rested her head on the table, and would just stare off into space. If a group member asked for Liliana to contribute, she responded, "I don't know" or "whatever you think is fine" or would give a one-word answer.

It turns out Liliana had similar responses when she was in music class and out at recess. During music she would sit in the corner, sometimes with her hoodie pulled over her head and sometimes with her hands over her ears. She required constant prompting to respond to questions and to engage with the instruments. "I just don't like music, is all," she would reply when the teacher asked what was wrong. However, that was not true because she could be seen wearing headphones with music playing when she walked to and from school each day. At recess she tended to play by herself or with a few friends who preferred quiet, more sedentary activities.

When the teachers met with Liliana's parents, a similar pattern emerged: group settings with a lot of people or noise tended to result in Liliana disengaging. Family gatherings, birthday parties, farmers' markets, and carnivals—none of them were things Liliana seemed to enjoy attending. They just figured she was more of an introvert and preferred to keep to herself.

The auditory overstimulation that Liliana experienced resulted in a nervous system response where she froze up and disengaged. She was so overwhelmed with the din during group work, or music class, or recess that she disconnected in order to protect herself. However, when auditory input was more controlled, like during classroom instruction or listening to her own music, Liliana could remain regulated and engaged. Let's look further into the auditory system and explore some strategies to help support Liliana—and students like her—at school.

What is the Auditory System?

Auditory input *is what we hear.* School is filled with auditory input "from the teacher, announcements over the loudspeaker, the hum of the air conditioner, conversations with peers, echoes in the gymnasium, a cacophony of instruments in music class, or hearing your name being called. Most of the classroom instruction provided at school comes in the form of auditory input."[1]

As shown in the diagram, auditory input is received by the eardrum and then processed in the temporal lobes of the brain. There are certain muscles (the stapedius and tensor tympani) in our ears that are responsible for allowing certain frequencies to pass through. If these muscles are weak then too much noise (typically lower frequencies) will end up passing though, which can then make it much more difficult for our brain to filter

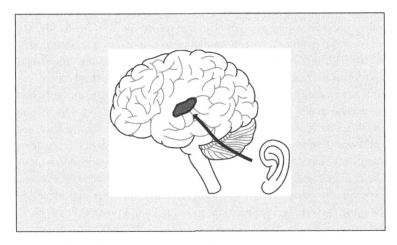

Figure 5.1 The Auditory System

Sensory input for the auditory system is received by the ear and then transmitted to the auditory cortex in the temporal lobes for processing.

out information. The higher frequencies associated with the human voice tend to get lost among the lower frequencies.[2] This can impact attention, focus, learning, and regulation. Consider, for a moment, if a student's brain struggles with filtering out low frequency auditory input and all they can hear is the hum of the air conditioner, the dripping water in the fish task, or the buzzing of the fluorescent lights. This will make it increasingly more difficulty for them to focus on the relevant auditory information they need in order to learn, such as attending to someone calling their name, listening to directions, or understanding what is being said.[1]

Typically sounds that are of lower frequencies and volumes, and that are somewhat rhythmic, are more relaxing and regulating. Think of listening to the soft crash of ocean waves along the shore, the sound of rain, or the soothing sound of a new mom singing a lullaby to her baby. Sometimes just imagining these sounds helps to decrease our sense of stress and nervous system arousal. On the other hand, higher frequencies and louder volumes can be energizing. Sudden and intermittent sounds, like a car alarm or fire alarm, also tend to be more stimulating. Depending on what we need in the moment, we can adjust the type of auditory input to either help us relax and calm down or allow us to become more energized and alert. The eardrum also does this automatically, by contracting the stapedius and tensor tympani muscles, when something is perceived as too loud. This decreases the load placed on the brain and decreases the likelihood that the amygdala will trigger a threat response.

We use auditory input to hear what someone is saying to us as a primary means of communication, which is important for our social engagement. The facial nerves that influence our facial expressions also influence our vocal tone and ability to listen.[2] This means that when we are happy and engaged with someone our voice sounds different than when we are anxious or angry. It also means that we listen better when we are happy and engaged compared to when we are anxious or angry. Researchers suggest that people who have compromised ability to listen—such as when we are tired, stressed, anxious, or under threat—also have compromised ability to engage in social communication.[2]

Interestingly, different languages also have different ranges of frequencies which can actually impact what sounds we hear.[3] Certain people actually have an "ear for language" based on this concept. Teachers in multi-cultural, bi-lingual, or English as a second language (ESL) classes should be aware that these differences in frequencies may influence how a student is learning. Similarly, some students may have more difficulty understanding a teacher from a different region or country who speaks with an accent.

Often the auditory system works in conjunction with the vestibular system to enhance our spatial awareness and maintain our balance because both are processed in the ear. Auditory input helps establish our spatial awareness through sonar tracking. **Sonar tracking** *is what we use to determine how near or far something is in relation to us.* Usually we attribute this skill to animals like bats and dolphins, but it is something that we do unconsciously as humans every day.[4] Think about when you're driving in your car and you hear an ambulance—before you even see it you can determine the general direction it is coming from and when it is getting closer. This skill is also used when finding our way in the dark. Students may use sonar tracking to anticipate a peer approaching from behind at recess.

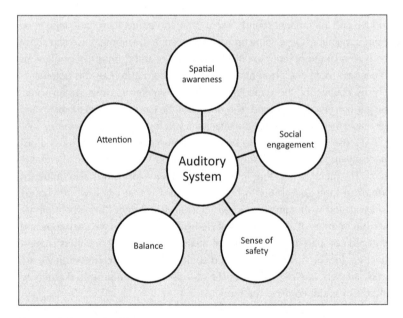

Figure 5.2 Supportive Diagram

The auditory system plays a critical role in how a child is responding to the environment and communicating with others. The diagram outlines the primary ways in which the auditory system impacts us on a regular basis.

Auditory processing is different than the ears being able to hear. Some people may have normal hearing in terms of frequencies and volumes, but may still struggle with processing auditory information. **Auditory processing** *refers to the "complex, higher-level cognitive skills that rely on the integration of auditory input and language skills."*[1] Auditory processing helps us to figure out what listen to and what to ignore. It helps us to remember instructions we hear or focus on the sequence of events in stories. It also helps us to interpret social language and recognize subtle differences between words.[5]

How does the Auditory System Impact Regulation and Learning?

The auditory system serves as a window to our ability to interact with others. As we know, interacting with peers and teachers is a huge aspect of learning. Our ability to listen also reflects our ability to verbally communicate. Students who feel regulated due to the tone, volume, and facial expressions of the teacher will be more apt to reciprocate social engagement and participate in the learning process.[2] If a student feels under threat due to social cues they are receiving from a teacher—loud volume, strained voice, tense facial expression—then their nervous system will shift to a state of regulation that makes it more difficult to take in auditory information.

Loud sounds also often jeopardize our sense of safety. When we are angry we yell. When someone cuts us off in traffic we honk our car horn. When the fire alarm sounds it can be deafening. The person on the receiving end of these noises often detects threat and is put on high alert. For students who may be more sensitive to sounds or have difficulty filtering out important sounds, like the teacher's voice, their nervous systems are likely working hard to stay regulated in order to maintain a feeling of safety that is important to learning. Oftentimes auditory processing differences can be an indication of another learning difference as well, such as ADHD, or ASD, language delays, or dyslexia.[6]

Here are several examples of common classroom activities that require a high level of auditory processing:

- *Following instructions*

  Following instructions uses many cognitively complex auditory processing skills. Amidst all the activity that occurs in a classroom—the rustling of papers, the shifting of peers in their seats, the hum of an air conditioner or heater, the buzzing of fluorescent lights—a student must be able to home in on the sound of the teacher's voice. This requires a high level of attention and figure-ground awareness, or the ability to pick out a particular sound amidst a background of other sounds. Then the student must discriminate what the teacher is saying and remember the multi-step directions that have been given. This process often happens very quickly and seamlessly without much conscious awareness.

- *Engaging with peers*

  When students interact with each other they often rely heavily on the auditory system—as do we when we engage with others. The complexity of using the auditory system increases when the number of students in the group increases or the intensity of background noise increases. This is because the student must more actively attend to what is being said and fill in the gaps of communication if something is lost among the other sounds. Students can actively listen better when they are regulated, which is a critical component to reciprocating speech and picking up on social cues.

  The cafeteria or playground, for example, can be very disorienting when trying to engage with peers because of the cacophony of sounds constantly at play. The echoes of numerous voices bouncing off the walls in the cafeteria, along with the screeches of laughter, crunching of potato chips, rustling of food packaging, and yelling of cafeteria aides all must be filtered out to some degree in order to focus on the conversation at a particular student's lunch table. That can be exhausting, and quite overwhelming, for a student who is sensitive to auditory input!

- *Participating in music class*

  Music class contains a wide variety of volumes, frequencies, and sounds, all of which use the auditory system. Certain students may be more sensitive to the volume of noise, depending on how much the middle ear muscles flex to protect the ear drum. Other students may be more sensitive to the frequency of the music or instrument. If a student has perfect pitch then hearing music that is out of tune can be particularly straining. The din of sounds coming from a multitude of students can, therefore, be quite dysregulating. Because we typically respond better to active input (something we initiate ourselves) rather than passive input (something initiated by someone else), you may notice that some students feel comfortable making a lot of noise themselves (such as playing an instrument loudly or singing constantly) but feel uncomfortable when other students make a lot of noise.

We know that it may be difficult to determine, during the course of a busy day in a busy classroom, whether a student is overstimulated or understimulated with sensory input, or is having a difficult time discriminating sensory information. However, we want to provide you with some signs to look out for and behaviors to consider. The important thing is that you are being curious about why a student may be demonstrating different behaviors or presenting with challenges in their learning. If you have more questions you can certainly reach out to the occupational therapist on staff at your school.

Here we expand upon signs taken from our book *The "Why" Behind Classroom Behaviors: Integrative Strategies for Learning, Regulation, and Relationships,* in order to help you determine if there is a pattern of challenges that may indicate a sensory processing disorder.

When a student's auditory system is *understimulated* you may see the following:

- Has a delayed response to name being called
- Must use touch to get the student's attention
- Misses parts of instructions given or often asks for instructions to be repeated
- Makes noises or sings to self in quiet environments
- Seems to "zone out"
- Asks for music to be turned on or turned up
- Talks out of turn
- Frequently engages in conversation with peers during class
- Talks loudly
- Speaks in a monotone voice

Experience It!—Auditory Overstimulation

Print out a medium or hard Sudoku puzzle to complete. While completing the puzzle, have the following auditory input in the background: 1) Music playing, 2) A school bell sounding every two minutes, 3) Muffled conversations, 4) Someone requesting you to do something.
Reflect on the following questions afterwards:

1) How did this compare with how you typically experience background noise?

2) What did you have to concentrate on more/less while completing the puzzle?

3) Were you only thinking about completing the puzzle or were you trying to discern the lyrics of the song, the conversation topic, or what was being asked of you?

4) Which sound was the most distracting to you?

This scenario is designed to help you better understand what a student with overstimulation to auditory input might experience on a regular basis. All of these sounds are amplified for them which makes it harder to filter them out and concentrate on the task at-hand.

When a student's auditory system is *overstimulated* you may see the following:

- Covers ears in loud environments
- Easily upset or runs away in loud environments, such as music class or the cafeteria
- Remains in a heightened state after a sudden, loud noise (such as after a fire drill or an announcement on the loudspeaker)
- Difficulty engaging in conversations in large groups
- Gets overly excited in large groups, such as in the cafeteria or at recess
- Makes noises to drown out other sounds
- Frequently asks students to be quiet or stop talking
- Seems "on guard" and anticipating noises
- Avoids eating crunchy foods because they are too noisy

When a student's auditory system cannot *discriminate* you may see the following:

- Confuses similar-sounding words easily when speaking or listening (e.g., bog/dog)
- Poor ability to adjust volume of voice, such as whispering
- Has a difficult time learning new songs
- Difficulty following multi-step directions
- Often asks for instructions to be repeated
- Gets lost when trying to follow a conversation, especially with more than one peer
- Does better following instructions or engaging socially in 1:1 or small group situations
- Has difficulty identifying the source of a sound (e.g., turns in the opposite direction to see where the person is standing)
- Seems to listen better in quiet places, like the library, compared to loud places, like the cafeteria
- Struggles to put different concepts together, especially when presented orally
- Does not differentiate similar sounding noises, such as a knock at the door or a hammer pounding

Note: Lack of auditory discrimination often indicates an auditory processing difference that may need to be evaluated by an audiologist.

Sensory-Smart Auditory Strategies for Every Classroom

After determining a particular student's response to auditory input, it's important to have some strategies in your back pocket to help support those needs. As teachers, we know you have so much to consider and so many students to support. Remember that you can always reach out to your school's occupational therapist for more help; these strategies are not meant to replace additional therapy. However, implementing some of these strategies can help

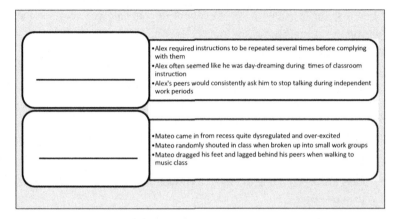

Figure 5.3 Interactive Scenario

Read the stories about students below that describe *patterns* the teacher has observed over several months. Determine if the student is experiencing difficulty with auditory understimulation, overstimulation, or discrimination.

the overall regulation and learning of the majority of students in your class. Through attending to your nonverbal cues, monitoring your tone of voice, and maintaining a calm presence with your students you will send them a message of safety and comfort while also supporting their sensory needs.[1] In the opening vignette Liliana's music teacher might approach her and say, "I know you like listening to music because I see you wearing headphones on your way home from school sometimes. I wonder why music class is different than when you listen to music on your own? Maybe we can find some solutions that will help you feel more comfortable in my class?"

Just like anything new, progress takes time; making new neural connections takes time. Give each strategy a few weeks to see how your students respond and adapt to the changes you make, then reassess what may need to be adjusted. There may be a combination of strategies that a student may need, which often requires a trial and error process.[1] Try not to get discouraged if only small changes are seen; these are important neurological stepping stones towards a larger goal. For example, Liliana might engage in the first and last 10 minutes of music class without any signs of dysregulation. In the following weeks she might increase this to 12 minutes and then 15 minutes. Or she might use noise-cancelling headphones for the entire class and then decrease to 40 minutes then 30 minutes then only for times when all the students are singing or playing instruments at once. Both of these options are helping Liliana increase her capacity to participate while allowing her to feel safe doing so.

Here we expand upon strategies taken from our book *The "Why" Behind Classroom Behaviors: Integrative Strategies for Learning, Regulation, and Relationships,* in order to support students with their auditory processing.

To promote appropriate auditory processing *for all students:*

- Be conscientious of your own volume level and cadence when talking
- When giving instructions, talk slowly, pause before repeating them, and repeat the instructions the same way. This will help all students better process the input
- Try to minimize environmental sounds within the classroom. This includes pencil sharpeners, fluorescent lights, and fans, to name a few
- Have several pairs of noise-cancelling headphones for students to access whenever needed
- Wear shoes that don't make clicking noises when you walk
- Check for understanding throughout a lesson
- Be thoughtful about which students sit near each other in the classroom or in the cafeteria

To provide *more* auditory input for *understimulation*:

- Encourage the student to sit in the front of the class
- Allow the student to listen to music through headphones during independent work time
- Play classical music during independent work time to increase attention
- Use visual input (like picture schedules or written instructions) to support what is being said
- Allow the student to sit away from other peers during independent work time in order to hum or tap a pencil
- Allow the student to sit away from other peers during silent reading time in order to read aloud
- Provide the student with enough time to respond

To provide *less* auditory input for *overstimulation:*

- Seat the student away from windows and doors
- Seat the student away from students who tend to make more noise
- Play classical music during independent work time to help filter out the low frequency environmental din
- Allow the student to eat snacks or chew gum while working. This contracts the muscles in the ear to better filter out unwanted sounds
- Allow the student to sit in the "sensory nook" or "quiet corner" when doing focused work
- Consider starting a "lunch club" for students who get overstimulated with the noise in the cafeteria. This can be a small group of students who gather in a teacher's office or classroom in order to eat and socialize in an environment with low auditory stimulation
- Place rugs, carpets, or drapes in rooms with high ceilings to decrease the echoing sound
- Ask for advance notification of when fire drills will happen
- Encourage the student to describe what they are hearing

To help support difficulty with *discrimination:*

- Encourage the student to sit in the front of the classroom to facilitate lip reading
- Group with students who are less talkative
- Use visual input (like picture schedules or written instructions) to support what is being said
- Break up instructions into smaller parts and have the student repeat the instructions aloud
- Encourage the student to describe what they are hearing
- Use descriptive and directional language when giving instructions
- Provide the student with enough time to respond

Note: Difficulty with auditory discrimination often indicates an auditory processing difference that may need to be evaluated by an audiologist.

Special Accommodations in Music Class to Consider for Children with Auditory-based Challenges

- Allow the student to wear noise-cancelling headphones
- Let the student direct when the music will start and stop to provide a greater sense of control
- Open a door or a window to diffuse some of the sound
- Provide the student with an instrument that has lower frequencies or a quieter volume
- Split up songs into smaller, more memorable parts for the student to learn more readily
- Send home music two to three days in advance for the student to become familiar and practice learning
- Encourage the student to imitate different beats and rhythms before putting them together in a song
- Use a metronome to help keep the student on beat

Reflective Activity

Ways I already support the auditory systems of my students	• •
New ways that I can support the auditory systems of my students	• •
Students who may need additional auditory-based support	• •
Ways I notice that I process auditory input	• •

Now that you know more about the auditory system and its impact on learning and regulation, think about how you can apply this information to your classroom.

References

1. Chaves, J., & Taylor, A. (2020). *The "Why" behind Classroom Behaviors: Integrated Strategies for Learning, Regulation, and Relationships*. Thousand Oaks, CA: Corwin.

2. Porges, S. (2017). *Safe and Sound Protocol Training, Continuing Education Course*. Aurora, CO: Integrated Listening Systems.

3. Doidge, N. (2016). *The Brain's Way of Healing: Remarkable Discoveries and Recoveries from the Frontiers of Neuroplasticity*. New York: Penguin Books.

4. Rosenblum, L. (2011). *See What I'm Saying: The Extraordinary Powers of Our Five Senses*. New York: W. W. Norton & Co.

5. Edell, H., Lucker, J. R., & Alderman, L. (2012). *Don't You Get It? Living with Auditory Learning Disabilities*. Sarasota, FL: First Edition Design Pub.

6. Iliadou, V., Bamiou, D. E., Kaprinis, S., Kandylis, D., & Kaprinis, G. (2009). Auditory processing disorders in children suspected of learning disabilities: A need for screening?. *International Journal of Pediatric Otorhinolaryngology, 73*(7), 1029–1034.

6 The Vestibular System

"Charlie, please sit up on the rug. You need to sit criss-cross so that your neighbors have enough space to learn too." This seemed to be a phrase Ms. Stanley said on a regular basis to Charlie. She had basically given up on him sitting in his chair at his desk because her repeated requests for him to stay sitting were disruptive to the entire class. He would stand, sit on one leg, rock back and forth, and sometimes even slide out of his chair. Classmates seated around Charlie were often distracted by his constant movement. Not to mention that Charlie often did not complete his work and had a difficult time paying attention to the teacher.

Ms. Stanley knew that Charlie was not doing this on purpose because she recognized that Charlie wanted to do well in class and expressed frustration that he had to keep bringing extra work home that he didn't finish at school. Yet she did not know how to support Charlie's constant moving around in class. And she was noticing that Charlie's movements would trigger dysregulation in her when she saw him changing positions during times of teacher instruction. Was Charlie doing this in other classes too? Did his parents notice this behavior at home?

Given that Charlie's movement-seeking behaviors in the class were clearly impacting his learning, the engagement of other students, and Ms. Stanley's regulation, it was important that Ms. Stanley continue to ask questions and seek support for Charlie. In this case, understanding how Charlie processes vestibular input is a key piece of the puzzle. As we will explore in this chapter the vestibular system has a huge impact on how we take in and process a wide variety of information. This difficult-to-say, often overlooked or unknown sensory system is one that demands the attention of educators across all ages.

What is the Vestibular System?

Vestibular input *is "how we detect movement, understand our relationship to gravity, and regulate our attention level."*[1] In school this may include tasks like "sitting upright in a chair, regaining balance when accidentally bumped by a peer, rock climbing in PE class, or staying in one place during circle time."[1]

As seen in the diagram, vestibular input is received by the vestibular apparatus in the inner ear and then processed in the cerebellum and the sensorimotor area. The vestibular system also has projections to the reticular formation and vestibular nuclei for eye movements. We use information from the vestibular system to facilitate movement of our body. Balance, muscle tone (how floppy or rigid our muscles are), and motor control are primary functions of the cerebellum, while motor coordination, posture, and position in space are primary functions of the sensorimotor area.[1] However, there

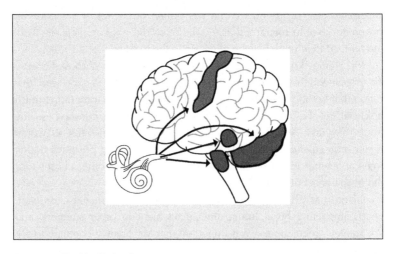

Figure 6.1 The Vestibular System

Sensory input for the vestibular system is received by the vestibular apparatus in the inner ear and then transmitted to the sensorimotor cortex and cerebellum for processing. It also has projections to the reticular formation and vestibular nuclei for eye movements.

is close communication between the cerebellum and sensorimotor area because all of these functions overlap. We rely on this system to facilitate all those important milestones in the first year of life that set the foundation for more complex movements: rolling, sitting up, reaching for objects, crawling, banging objects together, standing up, feeding oneself, and walking.

The receptor of vestibular input—the vestibular apparatus—is comprised of the semi-circular canals, the utricle, and the saccule. The semi-circular canals respond to rotational movement and changes in head position, such as spinning in a circle, riding a rollercoaster, hanging upside-down, and nodding your head. These types of vestibular movement tend to be more stimulating. Within the canals there is fluid that moves in response to the head's movement, allowing us to stay balanced and maintain our orientation in space. The utricle and saccule respond to linear movement and our relationship to gravity, such as riding in a car, rocking back and

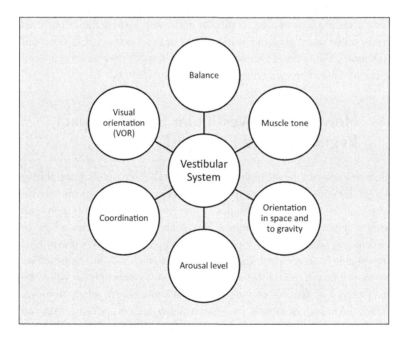

Figure 6.2 Supportive Diagram

The vestibular system plays a critical role in how a student is understanding their body and environment. The diagram outlines the primary ways in which the vestibular system impacts us on a regular basis.

forth, and lying down. These types of vestibular movement tend to be more calming. Within these structures there are hair cells that are displaced, or bent, depending on the degree and acceleration of movement.

The vestibular system also regulates our attention and arousal level. This is done through communication with an area in the brainstem called the reticular activating system (RAS). *The RAS is not only important in moderating alertness and posture, but also in helping you to habituate to repetitive, meaningless information that is not immediately important.*[2] Students who shift position in their seats or change position on the carpet are activating the RAS in order to regain focus and wake up the brain.[1] This is an important thing when you are maintaining your attention on a specified task. If the vestibular system is not sending enough information to the RAS this can result in hyperactive and distracted behaviors as a means to compensate.[2]

As mentioned in Chapter 4, another more complex role of the vestibular system is that of the vestibulo-ocular reflex (VOR). As a reminder, this interaction between the vestibular and visual system allows our eyes to stay stable when our head moves or for our head to stay stable when our eyes move. This is critical for our orientation in space and balance, as well as our ability to engage in reading and writing activities.

How does the Vestibular System Impact Regulation and Learning?

You can think of the vestibular system as the GPS (i.e., global positioning system) for your body.[3] Just as a GPS connects a computer to a car to assist in spatial directions, the vestibular system connects your brain with your body to help with spatial awareness. The vestibular system guides our motor movements, tells us when we need to speed up or slow down, prevents us from getting in an accident, keeps us focused on the road, and helps us find the most efficient route.[3] Without this important connection we would be completely lost, feel out of control, and not know how or where to move. In fact, the mother of sensory integration theory, Jean Ayers, noted that, "all other types of sensation are processed in reference to this basic vestibular system."[2] As you can imagine, the vestibular system plays a vital role in a student's engagement in the learning process.

Here are several examples of common classroom activities that require a high level of vestibular processing:

- *Sitting upright*

  Maintaining a stable, upright position in a chair or on the ground requires that the vestibular system is sending signals to the brain in order to have appropriate muscle tone, balance, and motor control. The vestibular system helps to engage the right muscles at the right time which is important for feeling grounded and trusting your body. Our equilibrium reactions that help us detect when we are falling and adjust our posture accordingly are critical to stability when sitting—these reactions rely on adequate information from the vestibular system. Appendix D has a variety of supportive seating options that may be appropriate for a student who demonstrates difficulty sitting upright.

- *Paying attention*

  As mentioned, vestibular-based signals to the reticular activating system (RAS) help to inform us about our level of alertness. In a calm, alert state we do our best learning. Being attentive also requires that we can filter out irrelevant information, habituate to unimportant stimulation, and only focus on what is important at the time. When we do start to unconsciously or consciously notice our attention slipping away, we need appropriate strategies to engage the vestibular system (slight shift in position, crossing our legs, moving our head in a circle, swiveling slightly in a chair) in order to regain attention—most students do this naturally.

- *Participating in PE class*

  Physical education actively engages the vestibular system more than any other class at school. In particular, balance and coordination-based activities like standing on one foot, jumping jacks, learning dance steps, jumping rope, imitating poses, riding a bicycle, and climbing all require good processing of vestibular input. The vestibulo-ocular reflex (VOR), as mentioned above, is important in PE class to help maintain a stable visual field when running so you don't feel like everything is bouncing up and down constantly. The VOR also plays an important role in eye-hand coordination so that the body can follow a ball through the air and then move towards a ball to catch it without losing balance or losing track of the ball.

- *Playing at recess*

  Similar to physical education, recess also provides many opportunities to engage the vestibular system. Swinging, going down the slide, running, riding a tricycle or bicycle, climbing the play structure, jumping, and sitting on a see-saw all tend to activate the linear vestibular system more than the rotary vestibular system. Hanging upside-down on the monkey bars, sitting on a merry-go-round, spinning in a circle, doing somersaults, and rolling down a hill all tend to activate the rotary vestibular system more than the linear vestibular system. Most children naturally engage in activities that help them balance the linear and rotary systems, which is why unstructured free play at recess can be regulating for the majority of students. Recess helps to "reset" the attentional system that is necessary to engage in the learning process.

- *Reading and writing*

  Both of these activities tend to be done in a seated position that requires appropriate signals from the vestibular system. In order to filter out distracting input and focus on the reading or writing task the RAS needs to be receiving appropriate information from the vestibular system. The vestibular system plays an important role in the motor movements involved in the writing process as well as holding the pencil in an appropriate position against gravity. Additionally, the VOR plays an important role in both reading and writing activities in order to maintain a stable visual field while the head and/or body is moving. When copying from the board the VOR helps the eyes make a smooth transition from looking up to looking back down.

We know that it may be difficult to determine, during the course of a busy day in a busy classroom, whether a student is overstimulated or understimulated with sensory input, or is having a difficult time discriminating sensory information. However, we want to provide you with some signs to look out for and behaviors to consider. Stay curious about why a student may demonstrate different behaviors or present with challenges in their learning. If you have more questions you can certainly reach out to the occupational therapist on staff at your school.

Here we expand upon signs taken from our book *The "Why" Behind Classroom Behaviors: Integrative Strategies for Learning, Regulation, and Relationships,* in order to help you determine if there is a pattern of challenges that may indicate a sensory processing disorder.

When a student's vestibular system is *understimulated* you may see the following:

- Changes positions constantly in chair and on rug
- Moves around when standing in line or cannot be still in one place
- Prefers to lean against objects or lie on the floor
- Does not seem to get dizzy
- Poor safety awareness on the playground
- Decreased balance, seems clumsy
- Difficulty with coordination activities in PE class
- Low muscle tone ("floppy" body)
- Fatigues easily
- Jumps from high surfaces on the playground
- Has difficulty maintaining attention, especially with seated activities
- Eye-hand coordination is poor, such as catching a ball or writing

When a student's vestibular system is *overstimulated* you may see the following:

- Prefers sedentary activities
- Gets upset when someone bumps them from behind
- Shows increased caution when climbing the play structure
- Avoids the swings and slides at recess
- Needs to hold the handrail when navigating stairs
- Clings to people or objects to feel more grounded
- Expresses fear of being in dark places, such as the classroom without lights turned on
- Avoids sitting or standing on unstable surfaces
- Gets easily dysregulated with movement activities during PE or at recess
- Wants to have their feet firmly planted on the ground
- Complains about tummy aches, headaches, and/or dizziness
- Moves slowly and cautiously in crowded environments, such as the gymnasium or auditorium

Experience It!—Vestibular Overstimulation

Stand on a soft pillow, balance board, or squishy/uneven surface while putting on socks. Try this activity with a variety of socks: ankle socks, tube socks, dress socks, sports socks.

Reflect on the following questions afterwards:

1) How did this compare with how you typically put on socks?
2) What did you have to concentrate on more/less while putting on your socks?
3) Were you only thinking about putting on socks or were you thinking about other aspects of your day?
4) Which type of socks were easiest to put on in this situation?

This scenario is designed to help you better understand what a student with sensitivity to vestibular input might experience on a regular basis. They feel changes in movement more readily than other people, resulting in discomfort and more awareness when having to maintain balance or move their body in a certain way. Sitting in a chair where their feet are not on the ground may be unsettling, or getting bumped from behind may trigger a "fight or flight" response. Forget about focusing on anything else while trying to manage the vestibular input!

When a student's vestibular system cannot *discriminate* you may see the following:

- Falls out of chair
- Wants to lie down when sitting on the floor
- Trips when walking up the stairs
- Falls (more frequently than other peers) when climbing on the playground
- Poor balance, especially with eyes closed
- Unable to communicate with head orientation while eyes are closed
- Seems confused about where they are in space
- Easily disoriented when navigating the school

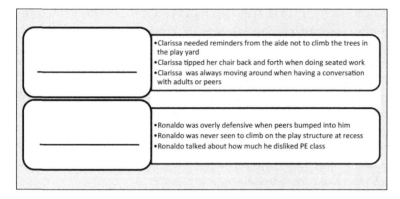

Figure 6.3 Interactive Scenario

Read the stories about students below that describe *patterns* the teacher has observed over several months. Determine if the student is experiencing difficulty with vestibular understimulation, overstimulation, or discrimination.

Sensory-Smart Vestibular Strategies for Every Classroom

After determining a particular student's response to vestibular input, it's important to have some strategies in your back pocket to help support those needs. As teachers, we know you have so much to consider and so many students to support. Remember that you can always reach out to the school occupational therapist for more help; these strategies are not meant to replace additional therapy. However, implementing some of these strategies can help the overall regulation and learning of the majority of students in your class. Through attending to your nonverbal cues, monitoring your tone of voice, and maintaining a calm presence with your students you will send them a message of safety and comfort while also supporting their sensory needs.[1]. In the opening vignette Ms. Stanley could tell Charlie, "Let's try something together that might help calm your body while you're sitting. If that doesn't work, we can keep trying until we find something that does work."

Just like anything new, progress takes time; making new neural connections takes time. Give each strategy a few weeks to see how your students respond and adapt to the changes you make, then reassess what may need to be adjusted. There may be a combination of strategies that a student may need, which often requires a trial and error process.[1] Try not to get discouraged if only small changes are seen; these are important neuro-logical stepping stones towards a larger goal. For example, Ms. Stanley might have an end goal of having Charlie sit for 20 minutes without being disruptive with his movements rather than the three to four minutes he currently sits. After having Charlie use a wobble stool for three days she notices that Charlie is now sitting for seven to eight minutes before he stands up and moves around—that's twice as long as before! While it's not quite where she wants him to be, as his nervous system continues to make positive connections and gets more of the vestibular input it needs, his cap-acity for seated attention will continue to grow.

Here we expand upon strategies taken from our book *The "Why" Behind Classroom Behaviors: Integrative Strategies for Learning, Regulation, and Relationships,* in order to support students with their vestibular processing. *Note: Vestibular input can have powerful, long-lasting effects on the brain and body, particularly rotational movement. Consult with an occupational therapist before implementing repeated or prolonged rotational movement with a student.*

To promote appropriate vestibular processing *for all students*:

- Integrate body breaks and movement activities into your schedule and curriculum. Stretching, yoga poses, jumping jacks, shaking "sillies" out, and walking around the classroom are all great! (See Appendix A for more ideas)

- Teach your students small movements they can do in their chairs when they start to notice their body getting restless or their attention waning. Ideas include: crossing then uncrossing your legs, moving your head in a circle, small wiggles back and forth on your butt cheeks, nodding your head up and down several times

- Provide alternative seating options for your students. Ball chairs, wobble stools, standing desks, and rocking chairs can all be helpful for particular students

- Make sure the chair height and desk height are appropriate for your students. Students should have chairs that allow their feet to be flat on the floor with hips and knees at 90 degrees (an "L" shape). The table or desk height should allow for the elbows to rest comfortably at a 90-degree angle

- Monitor the amount of homework you are giving in order to allow students to have adequate outdoor play time after school. Regulation through vestibular-based activities outside of school also impacts regulation during the school day
- Advocate for intermittent recesses throughout the school day and the need for regular PE classes

To help provide more *vestibular input* for *understimulation:*

- Encourage intermittent standing, even when doing desk work
- Use a vibrating pen or pencil
- Use a vibrating cushion on the chair
- Have the student use an alternative seating option (e.g., wobble stool, T stool, or ball chair)
- Use a core disc ("wobble cushion") on the chair or on the floor
- Allow the student to spin, seated on the teacher's chair, ten times in each direction
- Engage the student in chair stretches
- Engage the student in neck stretches and rolling the head in circular motions
- Enlist the student to perform various tasks around the class to provide more movement opportunities (e.g., pass out papers, wipe down the boards, run an errand)

To help provide *less* vestibular input for *overstimulation:*

- Allow the student to stand at the back of the line
- Avoid approaching or touching the student from behind because they may be fearful of becoming unbalanced
- Make sure the student's feet can be firmly planted on the ground when sitting in a chair; if not, provide a stool or phone book on which the student can place his feet
- Provide the student extra time to complete movement-based activities
- Allow the student to sit in a rocking chair during silent reading
- Allow the student to lie on the floor during independent work

- Encourage gentle swinging at recess

To help support difficulty with *discrimination*:

- Have the student use an alternative seating option (e.g., bean bag chair or chair with arms)
- Provide more support when sitting on a rug, such as a stadium seat, bean bag chair, or wall to lean against
- Allow the student to sit or lie on the ground when completing independent work
- Let the student stand near a wall or stabilizing surface when doing balancing activities
- Encourage the student to describe their body position

Special Accommodations in PE to Consider for Children with Vestibular-based Challenges:

- Send home exercises with the student a week in advance so they can practice them ahead of time
- Break down exercises into smaller component parts and anticipate that more practice will be necessary
- Place the student in a smaller group to minimize the movement happening around them
- Give the student more of a leadership role, such as being the referee, during whole-group activities (soccer, basketball, kickball, hockey) so they don't get lost in the mix
- Allow the student to stabilize him/herself against a surface when doing balance-related activities
- Roll the ball on the ground for the student to "catch"
- Give the student more breaks throughout the class

- Provide the student with extra proprioceptive input through the use of body weights (do not exceed 7–10% of the student's body weight)
- Engage the entire class in doing yoga poses or cross-body (a.k.a. midline crossing) activities: touch right elbow to left knee then left elbow to right knee; draw a large infinity sign in the air; rotate at the waist with arms out to the side like a helicopter
- Engage the entire class in the "superman" position (lie on the floor on your tummy with arms straight in front and legs straight in back; lift head, arms, and legs off the floor like you're flying and hold that position for as long as possible)

Reflective Activity

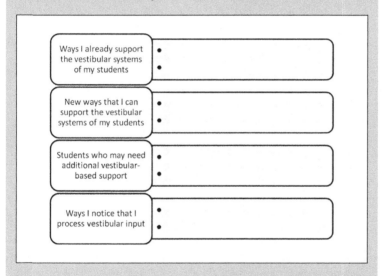

Now that you know more about the vestibular system and its impact on learning and regulation, think about how you can apply this information to your classroom.

References

1. Chaves, J., & Taylor, A. (2020). *The "Why" behind Classroom Behaviors: Integrated Strategies for Learning, Regulation, and Relationships.* Thousand Oaks, CA: Corwin.

2. Ayers, A. J. (2005). *Sensory Integration and the Child: Understanding Hidden Sensory Challenges.* Los Angeles, CA: Western Psychological Services.

3. Integrated Learning Strategies (April 2016). Vestibular system: Your child's internal GPS system for motor planning and attention. https://ilslearningcorner.com/2016-04-vestibular-system-your-childs-internal-gps-system-for-motor-planning-and-attention/ (Accessed August 2020)

The Tactile System

Jerome Jr., known as JJ, had notoriously bad handwriting ever since kindergarten. When JJ began second grade, his language arts teacher, Mrs. Williamson, had higher expectations for the legibility of his writing. She started to mark him down for responses she couldn't read. She didn't understand how he could hold his pencil with a fisted grasp, but he refused to try to hold it any other way. Mrs. Williamson did notice that JJ always selected a larger pencil with string wrapped around it—something he had made at a birthday party earlier in the year—when given the opportunity during "free write". While she resisted it at first, Mrs. Williamson observed that JJ had more legible writing when he used this pencil so she allowed it.

Writing wasn't the only thing with which JJ struggled. He lagged behind his peers when using scissors, too. He would chop off corners of the figures, leave too much white around the edges, or just go too fast. JJ still wore Velcro shoes even though almost all of his classmates had already learned to tie shoelaces. At times Mrs. Williamson heard JJ being teased for still wearing "baby shoes". She started to worry his decreased performance in these areas would start to negatively impact his self-esteem.

Maybe, thought Mrs. Williamson, JJ just needed more practice with fine motor skills like writing, cutting, and tying shoes. It's possible that he didn't focus enough on learning these activities outside of school. What Mrs. Williamson didn't know is that if the tactile system is not appropriately processing information it receives, then additional practice with these tasks will only go so far. It's important to look even further below the surface to understand why the tactile system contributes to success with these, and other, activities.

What is the Tactile System?

Tactile input *is what we feel when we touch something or when something touches us.* At school this might include "a teacher's hand on a student's shoulder, a hug from a peer, holding a pencil to write, playing in the sand box at recess, molding clay in art class, or the texture of the rug during circle time."[1]

As shown in the diagram, tactile input is received by the skin and processed in the sensorimotor cortex, primarily in the parietal lobe. Tactile input gives us an understanding about the texture and temperature of objects. We can detect if something is soft, hard, squishy, firm, rough, fuzzy, slimy, hot, warm, or cold just by using our sense of touch. This system also provides information about pain so we can protect our body, such as drawing our attention to our leg after we've fallen down so we can tend to a scrape.

Different parts of our body are more sensitive to touch input then others. A somatosensory homunculus, or body map, illustrates this. A **homunculus** *is a picture representation that delineates how different regions of the body respond to tactile input.* It can look quite strange at first because various

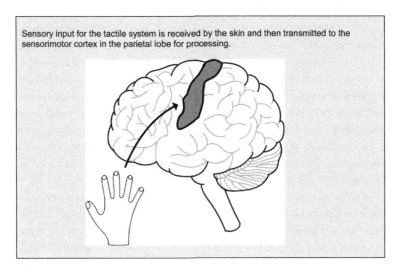

Sensory input for the tactile system is received by the skin and then transmitted to the sensorimotor cortex in the parietal lobe for processing.

Figure 7.1 The Tactile System

Sensory input for the tactile system is received by the skin and then transmitted to the sensorimotor cortex in the parietal lobe for processing.

body parts are drawn in different sizes depending on their sensitivity to tactile input; this makes the homunculus look a bit distorted. For instance, the hands and lips are quite sensitive to touch input while the elbow and toes are much less sensitive. This makes sense when we think about how much we use our hands and fingers to manipulate objects—we need all that tactile feedback in order to know what we are holding and that we are holding something correctly. Similarly, we want to make sure that whatever enters our mouth is safe to eat, so our lips naturally will be more sensitive in order to help us to better distinguish what we are putting into our mouth.

The tactile system pairs with the visual system—called the visuo-tactile system—to help us anticipate the texture of an object before we've touched it. This anticipation is based on previous tactile experiences throughout our life and has particularly strong foundations that are created during infancy and toddlerhood, which is why young children should be encouraged to explore with their hands. We expect that something with wood grains on it will be hard to the touch. We expect that something

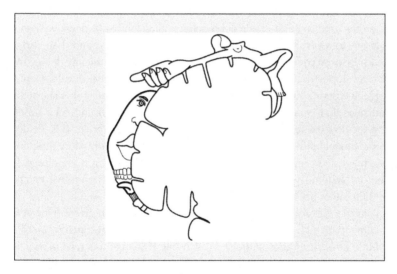

Figure 7.2 Somatosensory Homunculus

A homunculus is a picture representation that delineates how different regions of the body respond to tactile input. Some areas of the body are more sensitive to tactile input than others, such as the lips and fingers, which is why they appear to be quite large on the homunculus "body map".

liquid will be wet to the touch. When a particular texture does not match what we've perceived visually, it can be quite dysregulating.[2] For example, if you look at an apple and expect a firm texture—because that's what past experiences have informed you—but instead you pick it up and feel it squish in your hands because it's rotten, you might drop the apple quickly and screech, "Yuck!"

Experiencing a sense of physical safety and comfort around people and objects is largely related to how we process tactile information. Imagine feeling something sharp or rough; what emotions does this bring to mind? Now imagine holding something soft and fluffy; does this bring different emotions to mind? Emotions are often closely connected to touch, and the experiences we have around touch in infancy set the foundation for how we process this input. Think about an infant who is soothed when swaddled tightly, held skin to skin, or provided with a soft blanket. Such soothing tactile experiences help to regulate an infant's nervous system and facilitate the development of the brain, particularly when they are done within an attuned relationship. On the other hand, infants who experience medical complications, or preemies who spend their early months in the NICU, often undergo multiple medical procedures that can cause negative associations to touch for years.[3] Additionally, children who spend their early years in overcrowded orphanages may experience significant delays in the development of sensory processing, as well as language development, cognitive development, and overall physical development.[2,4] This research indicates that we all need positive sensory input, and in particular positive tactile experiences, not only to survive but also to thrive. This tactile nourishment helps to balance the brain's excitatory and inhibitory input to reach a state of regulation.[5] Interestingly, the tactile system is a reciprocal sensory system—you can both receive touch input from and give touch input to other people.[6]

In the classroom, it can be helpful to differentiate between types of tactile input and how it might be impacting students. **Light touch** is "tactile input that brushes against the skin."[1] Despite its name, this type of touch provides a large amount of stimulation which can often be dysregulating.[5] Recall a time that the tag on your shirt brushed against your skin. It's likely that you quickly rubbed on your neck to adjust the tag because it was bothersome. As you can imagine, this type of light touch may cause distractibility, irritability, or anxiety in some students to the degree that it impacts their ability to maintain a calm, alert state for learning.

Deep pressure touch, on the other hand, is *"tactile input that provides information about the muscles, joints, and tendons, and helps ground you and establish body awareness."*[1] Think about getting a massage, receiving a hug, or cuddling with something. This type of tactile input is often activated with the proprioceptive system (discussed in Chapter 8) and typically provides a great deal of calming input that gives us a sense of feeling grounded. Deep pressure touch can help to mask the negative sensation associated with pain or light touch.[5] Think about when you've walked through a spider web and it gently brushes against your skin uncomfortably. Typically the first response is to rub your arm repeatedly, not only to get the web off your skin, but also to help decrease your stress response.

We can experience tactile input as either passive or active. **Passive tactile input** *is touch that is imposed.*[6] This type of input tends to be stimulating, and potentially dysregulating, because it is out of our control or unexpected—so the brain responds protectively to discern how we need to act.[5] Think, for example, of when someone brushes up against you, or a tag rubbing against your neck (which is also light touch input), or the feeling of a bug crawling on your skin. Alternatively, **active tactile input** *is touch that is self-initiated.*[6] This type of input tends to be less dysregulating because you have control over it and are choosing to touch something. Examples include rolling clay, petting a dog, holding scissors, or eating a banana. One way to think about the way the brain responds to passive and active input is that "other people can tickle you, you can't tickle yourself";[5] this is because the brain does not need to protect you from yourself but it may need to protect you from someone or something else.

Tactile discrimination helps us differentiate what we touch, as well as what touches us. One type of tactile discrimination is **stereognosis**, or *the ability "to determine what we are touching without our vision."*[1] Students may use this to find a specified writing tool at the bottom of their backpacks or when digging for something in the back of a drawer. Another form of tactile discrimination is **graphesthesia**—*the ability to "perceive letters, numbers, and figures drawn on our skin without our looking."*[1] Poor tactile discrimination can negatively impact the way in which a student differentiates their fingers, resulting in poor fine motor skills, particularly in holding tools such as pencils, scissors, or silverware or manipulating objects such as blocks, buttons, or beads. Basically the student feels like they are constantly wearing gloves. This is the case with JJ in the opening vignette.

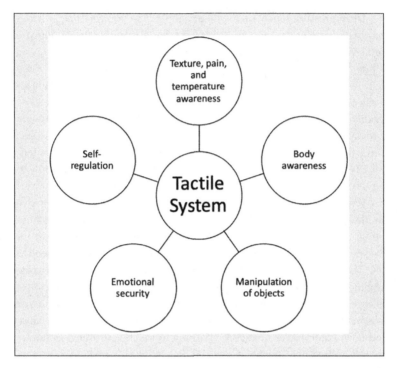

Figure 7.3 Supportive Diagram

The tactile system plays a critical role in how a child is developing an understanding of herself, her world, and the people around her. The diagram outlines the primary ways in which the tactile system impacts us on a regular basis.

How does the Tactile System Impact Regulation and Learning?

The tactile system serves as the foundation to explore our environment and body so that we can relate to others and start to manipulate objects. In fact, in utero, it is the earliest sensory system to functionally form.[2] Relationships serve as the foundation for our sense of trust, level of comfort, and feeling of safety. As we establish positive relationships through positive touch experiences, we develop an increased capacity to interact with other things around us.[5] We begin to develop an understanding of our own body as different from the body of our caregiver. Then we begin to develop an understanding of objects as different from our own body. This feeling of safety and ability to attend to new tactile experiences opens the door to picking up toys of varying textures which then leads to manipulating toys of varying textures. Eventually this matures to utilizing tools, like a spoon, crayons, and xylophone mallet—all precursors to more mature tools like scissors and a pencil. These experiences further enhance our understanding of our body and the world around us; something necessary to keep us regulated and engaged.

That said, students may find certain tactile experiences calming and soothing while others are more jarring or overwhelming. Some students may enjoy sitting closely to others, they may come in quickly for hugs, or seem to touch everything around them. Others, however, may prefer their personal space, not want to be hugged, and may be hesitant to touch sticky or other items such as glue, Play-doh, sand, or slime. Processing the sensation of touch can impact learning and regulation in many ways. Students, for example, who learn through touch often crave hands-on activities. They may be quick to jump into messy activities such as finger painting or playing in the sand box; or they may enjoy the physical contact of other peers. Students who may be sensitive or averse to certain tactile input may be more hesitant to engage in such activities; or they may prefer to keep their physical distance from peers. Striking a balance of tactile needs in the classroom can be one of the more challenging things to do as a teacher.

Here are several examples of common classroom activities that require a high level of tactile processing:

• *Writing*

  In order to hold a writing tool, like a pencil or pen, we need to feel comfortable with its texture on our fingers. If we cannot appropriately modulate that texture we will experience constant discomfort when writing. For some students the hard feeling of a pencil is actually painful. This is also true of the feeling of the paper on our hand and wrist as we move across the page to write. Some students may experience this sensation as akin to rubbing their skin across sand paper.

  We also use our tactile system to discriminate where our fingers need to be positioned on the writing tool. The feedback from the tactile system helps us "feel" our fingers appropriately in order to accurately move them. This helps us to hold the pencil in an appropriate way to increase the fluidity and legibility of our writing. If a student is not discriminating tactile input properly this can result in them being clumsy with their fingers and therefore using an immature or tight pencil grip in order to compensate.

- *Sitting or standing by peers*

As mentioned, passive touch and light touch can be more stimulating and more dysregulating to some students. When sitting on the rug during carpet time or standing in line, for example, these two forms of touch tend to be more prevalent. In these circumstances a peer might brush up against the student, put his hands too close to the student's face, accidentally step on the student's feet, or breathe heavily on the back of the student's neck. While these things may seem incidental, they can have negative outcomes for a student who is sensitive to this input.

Because the tactile system plays a large role in a student's body awareness, it is important for maintaining an appropriate distance from peers when sitting next to another peer or standing in line. A student who sits on top of, sits directly next to, or leans on another student might be wanting more tactile input to better understand their body.

- *Participating in art class*

The wide variety of tactile media present in art class provide an opportunity to explore different textures: from clay to paint to charcoal crayons to papier mâché. A student must be able to appropriately modulate these tactile sensory experiences so as not to get too overwhelmed or too excited. Another student might show more engagement when interacting with these more stimulating textures.

Art class also requires the use of many fine motor skills, including the manipulation of many tools. Students need good tactile discrimination in order to receive feedback about hand and finger movements, particularly when those movements require precision and dexterity. Crinkling up paper, drawing intricate details, rolling out clay; using paintbrushes, scissors, sponges—all of these rely on discriminatory information from the tactile system.

- *Eating with utensils*

Similar to writing, when we use utensils to eat we use our tactile system to determine how to appropriately hold them and manipulate them. Students might prefer to eat with their hands, or come with primarily finger food, in order to avoid the use of utensils. A student who struggles with utensils may consistently drop food on the floor when lifting the spoon to their mouth, require multiple attempts to spear their food with a fork, or tear food with their fingers because a knife is too challenging.

We know that it may be difficult to determine, during the course of a busy day in a busy classroom, whether a student is overstimulated or understimulated with sensory input, or is having a difficult time discriminating sensory information. However, we want to provide you with some signs to look out for and behaviors to consider. Maintain an open mind and a sense of curiosity about why a student may be demonstrating different behaviors or presenting with challenges in their learning. If you have more questions, you can certainly reach out to the occupational therapist on staff at your school.

Here we expand upon signs taken from our book *The "Why" Behind Classroom Behaviors: Integrative Strategies for Learning, Regulation, and Relationship,* in order to help you determine if there is a pattern of challenges that may indicate a sensory processing disorder.

When a student's tactile system is *understimulated* you may see the following:

- Seeks to touch things on a constant basis ("stop touching that!")
- Puts things in mouth to gain even more tactile input (remember the homunculus—the mouth is a big source of tactile input)
- Has poor personal space; sits or stands too close to others
- Wants to frequently hug, kiss, or touch other peers
- Frequently holds objects in hands
- Often fidgets with objects
- Puts hair in mouth or bites fingernails
- Loves touching shaving cream, sand, paint, glue
- Does not seem to notice or care when injured
- Leaves clothes twisted on body after using the bathroom

When a student's tactile system is *overstimulated* you may see the following:

- Bothered by messy textures; wants to wash hands frequently
- Only touches messy textures with fingertips
- Becomes anxious when sitting or standing near others

- Prefers the back or front of the line (or often stands out of line)
- Sits away from other peers; avoids large groups
- Dislikes or misbehaves during carpet time
- Shies away from social touch, such as a pat on the back, holding hands, or a hug
- Refuses to engage in certain art activities, like clay or papier mâché
- Wants to touch everything but does not want others touching him
- Frequently adjusts clothing, such as socks, shoes, neck of shirt, or pants waistband
- Tries to control games that involve touching, such as tag or touch football

When a student's tactile system cannot *discriminate* you may see the following:

- Constantly runs hands through same texture
- Unable to find something in bottom of backpack without looking
- Unable to find something in the back of a drawer without looking
- Difficulty counting on fingers
- Inefficient or immature grasp pattern on writing tools, utensils, or scissors
- Difficulty identifying where a body part has been touched without looking
- Poor fine motor skills, such as efficiency when using scissors, tying shoes, eating with utensils, fastening buttons
- Relies heavily on the visual system when doing eye-hand coordination tasks, such as writing, tying shoes, cutting, eating, and managing fasteners

Experience It!—Poor Tactile Discrimination

Find five or six different writing tools, such as a pencil, mechanical pencil, pen, marker, and highlighter, and place them in a bag. Put on a pair of gardening gloves. Reach into the bag to select 1) the mechanical pencil, then 2) the highlighter. Time how long each of these takes. Repeat the same activity without wearing the gardening gloves.

Reflect on the following questions afterwards:

1) How long did it take you to find the designated writing tools with the gloves on and with the gloves off?

2) How much more conscious effort was required when you completed the activity with the gloves on compared to the gloves off?

3) Which writing tool would be the easiest to find wearing gloves? Which would be the hardest?

4) Which writing tool would the easiest to write with while wearing the gardening gloves? Which would be the hardest?

This activity is designed to help you better understand what a student with poor tactile discrimination might experience on a regular basis. Discerning the properties of different objects, like texture, shape, and size, can be quite challenging for these students. Poor tactile discrimination not only impacts the identification of objects without the use of vision, but also the ability to appropriately hold a writing tool to perform precision movements like writing or drawing.

Sensory-Smart Tactile Strategies for Every Classroom

After determining a particular student's response to tactile input, it's important to have some strategies in your back pocket to help support those needs. As teachers, we know you have so much to consider and so many students to support. Remember that you can always reach out to the school occupational therapist for more help; these strategies are not meant to replace additional therapy. However, implementing some of these strategies can help the overall regulation and learning of the majority of students in your class. Through attending to your nonverbal cues, monitoring your tone of voice, and maintaining a calm presence with your students you

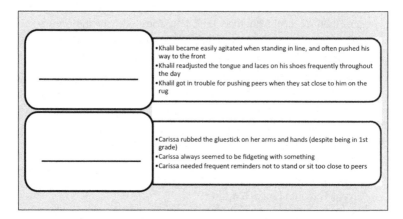

•Khalil became easily agitated when standing in line, and often pushed his way to the front
•Khalil readjusted the tongue and laces on his shoes frequently throughout the day
•Khalil got in trouble for pushing peers when they sat close to him on the rug

•Carissa rubbed the gluestick on her arms and hands (despite being in 1st grade)
•Carissa always seemed to be fidgeting with something
•Carissa needed frequent reminders not to stand or sit too close to peers

Figure 7.4 Interactive Scenario

Read the stories about students below that describe *patterns* the teacher has observed over several months. Determine if the student is experiencing difficulty with tactile understimulation, overstimulation, or discrimination.

will send them a message of safety and comfort while also supporting their sensory needs.[1] Mrs. Williamson, in the opening vignette, might say to JJ during writing time, "I notice that you really like that pencil with the string around it. Can you tell me what you like about it? I'm curious to help find ways to make handwriting feel less stressful."

Just like anything new, progress takes time; making new neural connections takes time. Give each strategy a few weeks to see how your students respond and adapt to the changes you make, then reassess what may need to be adjusted. There may be a combination of strategies that a student may need, which often requires a trial and error process.[1] Try not to get discouraged if only small changes are seen; these are important neurological stepping stones towards a larger goal. For example, Mrs. Williamson might have a goal of JJ writing seven legible sentences during "free write", similar to the other students. After providing him with a new pencil grip, JJ can now write five sentences (compared to his typical three sentences) with about 70% legibility. Several weeks later JJ is still writing five sentences but the legibility has increased to almost 90%. These step-wise improvements demonstrate that JJ is better supported.

Here we expand upon strategies taken from our book *The "Why" Behind Classroom Behaviors: Integrative Strategies for Learning, Regulation, and Relationship,* in order to support students with their tactile processing.

To promote appropriate tactile processing *for all students:*

- Let students approach you rather than you approaching them, particularly in the first several weeks of school. This will help you gauge students who like tactile input versus students who are less comfortable with tactile input

- Ask permission before touching a student on the shoulder, hands, or back—this form of light touch can be stimulating and potentially dysregulating

- Provide a soft rug with a high pile for students to sit on during carpet time

- Use a rug that has distinct places for students to sit

- Provide alternative seating options, such as a core disc or cushion, during circle time and seated activities for more comfort

To provide *more* tactile input for *understimulation*:

- Allow students to use fidget toys in the classroom. Note that not all fidget toys are beneficial or help facilitate improved attention, especially those that light up or make noise. Our favorites include: textured Tangle jr., flippy chain, Wacky Tracks, and Whatz It fidget

- Put Velcro under the desk for the student to rub

- Allow the student to rub feet on a textured piece of material placed under the desk

- Allow the student to wear a soft sweatshirt or vest, such as microfleece, in class

- Use a vibrating pen or pencil when writing

- Use a textured pencil, pen, or pencil grip when writing

- Encourage the student to "wake up" his body by rubbing his arms and legs quickly

To provide *less* tactile input for *overstimulation:*

- Allow the student to sit on a cushion during carpet time to provide more comfort

- Provide cushions or core discs (the Abilitations squellet is our favorite) to decrease the tactile input from hard chairs
- Encourage the student to engage in "heavy work" activities (body squeezes, chair push-ups, wall pushes, stretching, jumping) when they become dysregulated
- Allow the student to stand in the front of the line or back of the line
- Allow the student to sit on the front corner or back corner of the rug during carpet time
- Allow the student to keep something soft at their desk to rub (such as a stuffed animal)
- Use a basic, soft pencil grip to minimize tactile input from the hard pencil
- Provide gloves for the student to wear during messy tactile activities (e.g., molding clay, using glue, painting)
- Always approach the student from the front
- Offer alternatives to doing activities in a large group
- Consider allowing the student to remove shoes during classroom instruction, independent work time, or silent reading time (you will need to check with the school policies before doing this, as it may be a safety concern in case of an emergency)

To help support difficulty with *discrimination:*

- Provide Jumbo Grip pencils and/or pencil grips (the Grotto grip and Crossover grips are our favorite) for more tactile feedback when writing
- Use a vibrating pen or pencil
- Encourage the student to describe the texture of different materials used in the classroom
- Have the student use a transparent pencil box and backpack
- Do "heavy work" activities (pushing, pulling, jumping, stretching) before sitting down for desk work
- Do finger warm-ups before a fine motor activity, like touching each finger to the thumb or forming different numbers with the fingers

Special Accommodations in Art Class to Consider for Children with Tactile-based Challenges

- Allow the student to wear gloves
- Consider starting with dry textures then moving to wet textures
- Allow the student to partner with another student to complete the project
- Provide alternative tactile media, such as Model Magic instead of clay, to complete the same project
- Use larger paintbrushes and drawing pencils to make it easier for the student to grip
- Provide the student with adaptive scissors, such as loop scissors or spring scissors
- Allow the student extra time to complete the project

Reflective Activity

Ways I already support the tactile systems of my students	• •
New ways that I can support the tactile systems of my students	• •
Students who may need additional tactile-based support	• •
Ways in which I process tactile input	• •

Now that you know more about the tactile system and its impact on learning and regulation, think about how you can apply this information to your classroom.

References

1. Chaves, J., & Taylor, A. (2020). *The "Why" behind Classroom Behaviors: Integrated Strategies for Learning, Regulation, and Relationships.* Thousand Oaks, CA: Corwin.

2. Linden, D. J. (2015). *Touch: The Science of Hand, Heart, and Mind.* New York: Penguin Group.

3. Pineda, R., Guth, R., Herring, A., Reynolds, L., Oberle, S., & Smith, J. (2017). Enhancing sensory experiences for very preterm infants in the NICU: An integrative review. *Journal of Perinatology: Official Journal of the California Perinatal Association, 37*(4), 323–332. doi:10.1038/jp.2016.179

4. Lin, S. H., Cermak, S., Coster, W. J., & Miller, L. (2005). The relation between length of institutionalization and sensory integration in children adopted from Eastern Europe. *American Journal of Occupational Therapy, 59*(2), 139–147.

5. Ayers, A. J. (2005). *Sensory Integration and the Child: Understanding Hidden Sensory Challenges.* Los Angeles, CA: Western Psychological Services.

6. Burpee, J. (2015). *Sensory Integrative Intensive Continuing Education Course.* Medfield, MA: Educational Resources, Inc.

7. Chen, H. Y., Yang, H., Chi, H. J., & Chen, H. M. (2013). Physiological effects of deep touch pressure on anxiety alleviation: The weighted blanket approach. *Journal of Medical and Biological Engineering, 33*(5), 463–470.

8 | The Proprioceptive System

"Emilio, you don't need to use that much glue!," reprimanded Mr. Williams as he watched Emilio squeeze a large glob onto his paper. "We talked about that earlier today. If you're not going to listen then I'm going to need to take away the glue." Emilio shrunk back into his chair and then squeezed another quarter-sized glob of glue onto his paper. He looked up to see Mr. Williams glaring at him. "I didn't mean to! I'm not doing it on purpose," offered Emilio. But the deed was done. Emilio lost his privilege of using the glue the remainder of the day, which resulted in Emilio sulking around, wondering why his body didn't work like it was supposed to work.

The next day of kindergarten, Emilio was working on a project that required him to cut out the letter B. "Mr. Williams!," Emilio called, "I need another paper. Mine ripped again." As Mr. Williams handed Emilio his third letter B page he commented, "This is the last one you will get. Please stop goofing around and pay attention to what you're doing." Just like yesterday, Emilio wondered why his body didn't do what he wanted it to do. He wasn't trying to rip the paper; actually he was trying really hard not to rip it. But it just wasn't working.

Later that day, as the class lined up for lunch, Emilio locked his elbows and knees while marching in place like a toy soldier. As a result he accidentally hit a peer in front of him. Mr. Williams took notice. "Emilio, why do I need to keep reminding you to stand still in line? It shouldn't be that hard." Yet, for Emilio, it was. It felt much better to lock his elbows and knees while standing. It actually made standing in line easier. Why didn't the other kids need to do that too?

"Kindergarten is stupid," complained Emilio to his mom later that week. He continued, "Other kids just make fun of me and I'm not doing anything wrong. My body just doesn't work right." Emilio's mom knew he wasn't the most coordinated kid but she didn't realize how it was impacting his self-esteem. She had noticed that Emilio was constantly playing too rough with his little brother, slamming doors around the house, and accidentally breaking his toys.

What may look like a student who is intentionally using too much force, being too rough, or goofing around, like Emilio, is actually someone who is struggling to process proprioceptive input. Similar to the vestibular system, this odd term that is not well-known plays a critical role in how we understand our bodies. Learning more about the proprioceptive system will greatly benefit a wide range of students because of its impact on regulation overall.

What is the Proprioceptive System?

Proprioceptive input *is, essentially, our body awareness communicated via our muscles and joints.* It helps us to understand where our body is in space and how to move our bodies through that space.[1] It is reflected in activities such as "navigating the classroom, running across the playground, crossing the monkey bars at recess, sitting an appropriate distance from other peers during circle time, using appropriate pressure when writing, or imitating dance moves in PE class."[2]

As seen in the diagram, proprioceptive input is received by the muscles and joints and processed in the sensorimotor area and the cerebellum, among other areas in the brain. Proprioceptive information helps us detect force and vibration. **Grading of force** *is what allows us to adjust the amount of strength we use when lifting, pushing, pulling, or throwing objects*—something many of us do naturally before we even touch something.[3] For example, if we see a pitcher filled halfway with water we will automatically know to use less force than if the pitcher is filled all the way with water. **Proxy touch**, *or the ability to discern the texture of something by using a tool,* such as knowing what type of paper we are writing on or cutting through, is another phenomenon of the proprioceptive system that allows us to grade force.[3] "For example, we can *feel* that using a pencil on sandpaper is different than using a pencil on construction paper," so we know to use more force when writing on sandpaper.[2] However, pressing

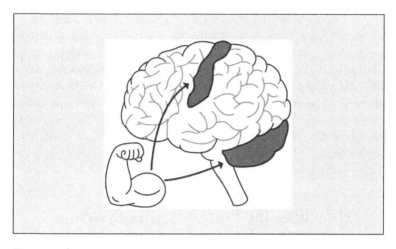

Figure 8.1 The Proprioceptive System
Sensory input for the proprioceptive system is received by the muscles and joints and then transmitted to the sensorimotor cortex and cerebellum for processing.

more firmly on the tool or surface decreases proxy touch perception.[3] This means students who grasp the pencil tightly or push hard when writing tend to use the same amount of force regardless of the paper being used, resulting in breaking the tip of the pencil or tearing the paper.

Input from the proprioceptive system, along with information from the tactile system, also determines *"how much we should move a certain body part and where that body part is located in relationship to other body parts"—called* **kinesthetic feedback**.[2] Kinesthetic feedback gives us a sense of our own body and how our body works as a unit. It helps facilitate our awareness of the right and left sides of our body. If we don't have a good sense of our own body then it is hard to gain a good sense of our environment or how we use various things within our environment.[4] You can think about eating cereal with your eyes closed—you know where your hand is in relationship to your mouth because of your proprioceptive system.

Due to the primarily inhibitory function of the proprioceptive system, this type of input tends to be more calming for the brain and body.[4] Most of the other sensory systems tend to provide a balance of excitatory and inhibitory signals. When overstimulation occurs, the inhibitory function activates the parasympathetic nervous system to bring the brain and body back into a state of regulation. This is precisely what happens during deep pressure input or "heavy work" activities, such as those that provide a pushing or pulling resistance to the muscles and joints. For students this may include wall push-ups, erasing whiteboards, carrying a backpack with books, or jumping up and down. Chewing or sucking on something also provides a large amount of proprioceptive input to the mouth; this will be discussed further in Chapter 9. Use of proprioceptive-based activities are, therefore, a ubiquitous and effective way in which a student can stay regulated throughout the stimulating school day, as well as calm back down after becoming dysregulated. This is one of the reasons why research supports the finding that students benefit from frequent outdoor recess breaks at school.[5,6]

How does the Proprioceptive System Impact Regulation and Learning?

Think about the proprioceptive system as the roots for our body—this system keeps us grounded. Students with poor proprioceptive processing feel lost without these roots. Just like roots enable a tree to gain stability, the proprioceptive system provides our brain with stable information about our muscles and joints. Without roots, or with roots that are poorly formed, a tree can topple over, not receive nutrients it needs, and struggle with producing fruit. Similarly, students with difficulty processing proprioceptive input can appear clumsy, not receive proper body awareness, and struggle with producing output.

The proprioceptive system works closely in conjunction with the vestibular system. Basically, vestibular input provides information about where the body moves while proprioceptive input provides information about how much the body moves. The proprioceptive system also works closely in conjunction with the tactile system, forming the somatosensory system, in order to enhance body awareness by connecting external sensation of touch with the internal sensation of muscle and joint position. So if you're noticing a lot of similarities between the proprioceptive, and vestibular and tactile systems, there's a reason why.

Here are several examples of common classroom activities that require a high level of proprioceptive processing:

* *Sitting upright*

    Sitting upright in a chair uses the proprioceptive system, along with the vestibular system, to provide information to the muscles about which

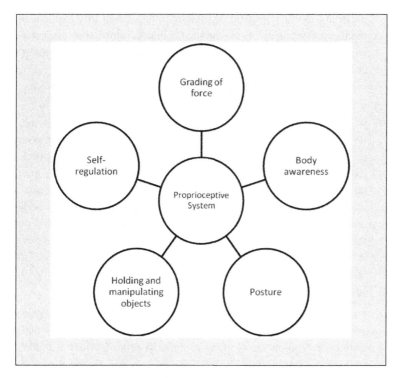

Figure 8.2 Supportive Diagram

The proprioceptive system is important for how we make sense of our own body, so we can, in turn, make sense of things outside of our body. The diagram outlines the primary ways in which the proprioceptive system impacts us on a regular basis.

muscles should be engaged and how much those muscles should contract. This system helps us make little adjustments to our posture when necessary to engage in activities without falling out of the chair. The proprioceptive system also influences our endurance for seated activities, as well as the ability to sustain attention (via the RAS discussed in Chapter 6). Appendix D has a variety of supportive seating options that may be appropriate for a student who demonstrates difficulty sitting upright.

- *Writing*

  The proprioceptive system—through grading of force, proxy touch, and kinesthetic feedback—helps a student determine how much pressure to use when holding a pencil and when pressing the pencil onto the paper. If too much pressure is used then the student may experience pain, express fatigue, or even rip the paper (this is true when erasing as well). If too little pressure is used then the student may be uncomfortable holding the pencil or unable to see what is written.

Proprioceptive input helps establish a hand dominance for holding a writing tool, differentiate between the left and right sides of the paper, and understand the directions required for learning strokes (up, down, left, right, top, bottom). It is purported that a student with poor proprioceptive processing pushes their pencil away from their body ("bottom-up approach") rather than pulling the pencil towards their body ("top-down approach") because they do not have a firm enough understanding of their body, so everything still moves from their body outward. When forming letters and numbers, a student also relies on the proprioceptive system to provide kinesthetic feedback about how it "feels" to form the letter D versus the letter M, for example. This also requires a high degree of praxis, which will be discussed in Chapter 10.

- *Playing at recess*

  Nearly every aspect of the playground involves the proprioceptive system. Students must have a good sense of their body and how their muscles and joints are working together in order to climb a ladder, traverse the monkey bars, kick a ball, chase a peer, or ride a tricycle. If a student feels they are not able to keep up with peers, is unknowingly being too rough with peers, or is perceived as clumsy, this can certainly wear on the student's self-confidence and self-esteem.

- *Participating in PE class*

  Throwing or kicking a ball with appropriate force, landing on two feet when jumping, maintaining body control when dancing, and sustaining certain body positions all rely heavily on information from the proprioceptive system. This system is also important for endurance—continued or repeated recruitment of muscles for a sustained period of time. Tiring easily or dragging around during PE class may indicate that the proprioceptive system is not adequately processing input.

We know that it may be difficult to determine, during the course of a busy day in a busy classroom, whether a student is overstimulated or understimulated with sensory input, or is having a difficult time discriminating sensory information. However, we want to provide you with some signs to look out for and behaviors to consider. The important thing is that you are being curious about why a student may be demonstrating different behaviors or presenting with challenges in their learning. If you have more questions you can certainly reach out to the occupational therapist on staff at your school. These signs are a way to help you determine if there is a pattern of challenges that may indicate an SPD.

Here we expand upon signs taken from our book *The "Why" Behind Classroom Behaviors: Integrative Strategies for Learning, Regulation, and Relationships,* in order to help you determine if there is a pattern of challenges that may indicate a sensory processing disorder.

When a student's proprioceptive system is *understimulated* you may see the following:

- Slouches when sitting in a chair or on the floor
- Seems to always be jumping or bouncing
- Loves crashing into people or objects
- Hangs on to other people or objects
- Locks joints when standing, jumping, or walking
- Seeks hugs or squishes
- Writes hard or messily
- Breaks writing tools or toys
- Fatigues easily
- Appears clumsy and accident prone
- Shows disinterest in fine motor activities; prefers gross motor play
- Bounces legs when sitting
- Chews on toys, pencils, or clothes

Experience It!—Proprioceptive Understimulation

Walk across the room to a specified location, such as a light switch or door knob, with your eyes open to turn on the light or open the door. Now repeat this action with your eyes closed. Walk to the specified location again with eyes closed but do so in a slightly zig-zag line.

Reflect on the following questions afterwards:

1) How did you rely on your body awareness to get you to the specified location?

2) How much more difficult was this activity when you couldn't walk in a straight line?

3) What conscious or sub-conscious strategies did you use to help get to the location when walking zig-zag?

This activity is designed to help you better understand how a student with proprioceptive understimulation might relate to their body. They might feel disoriented about where their body is in space and have a poor understanding of their body in relationship to itself. This can make them appear clumsy and, at times, aloof. They might stomp around to gain more feedback to their muscles so that they can be more aware of their own body and how their body is moving.

When a student's proprioceptive system is over*stimulated* you may see the following:

- Avoids jumping activities
- Pushes away from hugs
- Writes very lightly

Note: Typically overstimulation to proprioceptive input is not seen in children; it is more likely a sign that the vestibular system or tactile system is overstimulated. This, again, is because the proprioceptive system provides primarily inhibitory information to the brain, not excitatory information.

When a student's proprioceptive system cannot *discriminate* you may see the following:

- Falls out of chair because does not adjust posture
- Falls or bumps into objects
- Does not use the right amount of force to push, pull, grasp, or throw

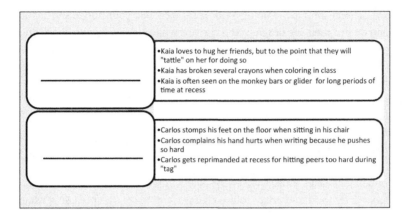

Figure 8.3 Interactive Scenario

Read the stories about students below that describe *patterns* the teacher has observed over several months. Determine if the student is experiencing difficulty with proprioceptive understimulation, overstimulation, or discrimination.

- Writes too hard or too light (or switches between the two)
- Delayed right/left awareness
- Seems unaware of his body in space
- Difficulty completing an age-appropriate drawing of a person (e.g., missing body parts, displaced body parts, disproportionate, poor use of detail)

Sensory-Smart Proprioceptive Strategies for Every Classroom

After determining a particular student's response to proprioceptive input, it's important to have some strategies in your back pocket to help support those needs. As teachers, we know you have so much to consider and so many students to support. Remember that you can always reach out to the school occupational therapist for more help; these strategies are not meant to replace additional therapy. However, implementing some of these strategies can help the overall regulation and learning of the majority of students in your class. Through attending to your nonverbal cues, monitoring your tone of voice, and maintaining a calm presence with your students you will send them a message of safety and comfort while also supporting their sensory needs.[1] Mr. Williams, in the opening vignette, could approach Emilio with his observations rather than criticisms. He might say, "Emilio, I notice you're having a hard time using the glue. It seems that you're squeezing the bottle so hard that too much glue is coming out." Or he could comment, "Emilio, I see that you're tearing the paper every time you use the scissors. Maybe you're pushing the scissors too hard along the paper. I wonder what we can do to prevent that from happening?"

Just like anything new, progress takes time; making new neural connections takes time. Give each strategy a few weeks to see how your students respond and adapt to the changes you make, then reassess what may need to be adjusted. There may be a combination of strategies that a student may need, which often requires a trial and error process.[1] Try not to get discouraged if only small changes are seen; these are important neurological stepping stones towards a larger goal. Mr. Williams, for example, could start by using cardstock for projects that required Emilio to cut out something. As Emilio gained confidence and received more feedback to his proprioceptive system, Mr. Williams might then transition to using construction paper. Eventually, two months later, Emilio may be ready to cut on copy paper. When Emilio needed to stand in line, Mr. Williams could offer up the idea of standing the front of the line while marching so he still got the proprioceptive input he needed without hurting other students. Alternatively, Mr. Williams might suggest that Emilio stand against the wall, pushing against it as needed, while waiting so he received proprioceptive input.

To promote appropriate proprioceptive processing *for all students:*

- When a student becomes overstimulated, suggest activities such as squeezing a stress ball, body squeezes, helping to carry something heavy, erasing the chalkboard or dry erase board, wall pushes, or jumping on the spot, as these tasks give sensory inputs which tend to be more calming.

- Teach students ways to give themselves calming, regulating proprioceptive input such as stretching, joint compressions, bear hugs, chair push-ups.

- Have bean bag chairs or stadium seats available for students to use during carpet time, particularly for students who have difficulty sitting upright.

- Advocate for intermittent recesses throughout the school day and the need for regular PE classes.
- Encourage the manipulation of materials and hands-on learning.

To provide *more* proprioceptive input for *understimulation*:

- Engage the student in gross motor movement before seated work: jumping up and down, chair push-ups, wall pushes, stretches, yoga
- Allow the student to sit in a bean bag chair during silent reading time
- Have the student use an alternative seating option (e.g., chair with arms or ball chair)
- Loop a TheraBand® (red or green resistance is best) around the front two legs of a chair for the student to put his feet in and stretch
- Allow the student to carry around or wear a backpack filled with books (keep to 7–10% of the student's body weight)
- Used a weighted blanket (keep at 7–10% of the student's body weight) or a core disc placed on the student's lap during circle time
- Ask the student to help with "heavy work" activities in the classroom: wiping down boards, taking down chairs, carrying books, pushing the lunch basket, opening the door for people, sharpen pencils manually
- Have the student wear a compression shirt and/or shorts

To help support a student's difficulty with proprioceptive *discrimination*:

- For students who press hard when writing, place a binder, folder, or other semi-squishy surface under the paper to provide additional feedback
- Use sand paper, chalkboards, tissue paper, and magnetic boards to practice writing on different surfaces
- Allow the student to carry around or wear a backpack filled with books (keep to 7–10% of the student's body weight)
- Ask the student to help with "heavy work" activities in the classroom: wiping down boards, taking down chairs, carrying books, pushing the lunch basket

- Use weighted objects/materials at recess and during PE
- Encourage the student to assess beforehand if they think an object will be heavy or light

Special Accommodations in PE to Consider for Students with Proprioceptive-based Challenges

- Use weighted balls to provide more feedback during throwing activities
- Use a weighted vest or compression vest to provide more feedback
- Engage the entire class in warm-up exercises that encourage strong feedback to the proprioceptive system: marching, jumping jacks, wall pushes, body squeezes, sit-ups, animal walks, yoga poses
- Have the student stand farther away or closer up to other students when throwing or kicking (depending on the student's grading of force)
- Break down activities into smaller components for the student to focus on individual movements
- Provide the student with more frequent breaks
- Allow the student to take an alternative role, such as being the referee, leader, music controller, clean-up crew, etc., when an activity becomes too challenging or fatiguing
- Provide the student with gentle reminders when you observe them locking their joints

Reflective Activity

Ways I already support the proprioceptive systems of my students	• •
New ways that I can support the propriocepive systems of my students	• •
Students who may need additional proprioceptive-based support	• •
Ways I notice that I process proprioceptive input	• •

Now that you know more about the proprioceptive system and its impact on learning and regulation, think about how you can apply this information to your classroom.

References

1. Ayers, A. J. (2005). *Sensory Integration and the Child: Understanding Hidden Sensory Challenges.* Los Angeles, CA: Western Psychological Services.

2. Chaves, J., & Taylor, A. (2020). *The "Why" behind Classroom Behaviors: Integrated Strategies for Learning, Regulation, and Relationships.* Thousand Oaks, CA: Corwin.

3. Rosenblum, L. (2011). *See What I'm Saying: The Extraordinary Powers of Our Five Senses.* New York: W. W. Norton & Co.

4. Burpee, J. (2015). *Sensory Integrative Intensive Continuing Education Course.* Medfield, MA: Educational Resources, Inc.

5. Hanscom, A. (2016). *Balanced and Barefoot: How Unrestricted Outdoor Play Makes for Strong, Confident, and Capable Children*. Oakland, CA: New Harbinger Publications.

6. Barros, R. M., Silver, E. J., & Stein, R. E. (2009). School recess and group classroom behavior. *Pediatrics, 123*(2), 431–436.

9 | The Gustatory, Olfactory, and Interoceptive Systems

"Avi, you just went to the bathroom 30 minutes ago. Sit back down. Stop trying to avoid your work," remarked Ms. Olsen. Avi retorted, "But I really need to go!" Only four weeks into the school year, Ms. Olsen had struggled with Avi constantly asking to use the bathroom—almost three times as frequently as any other student. Was he trying to avoid his school work? Was something going on at home? Was he being bullied by another student? Did he really need to pee *that* often?

Some days Ms. Olsen would oblige and let him go when he asked. Other days she would use humor to connect with him and "convince" him he didn't really need to go to the bathroom again. Today Ms. Olsen tried to place firm boundaries. "I'm sorry, Avi. You'll need to wait until you finish your work. You can't keep going to the bathroom." He hung his head and went back to his seat, only to find himself thinking about how much he needed to pee rather than thinking of factors of 4.

Avi's difficulties with urinating frequently were actually rooted in poor processing of interoceptive information. He did not have anything "wrong" medically and he wasn't avoiding his work. He just felt the need to urinate more readily than others, which made him feel like any strain on his bladder was an urgent need to use the bathroom. This obviously became a huge distraction for him in class when he wasn't allowed to go pee, but it was also a distraction to other students when he needed to pee so often.

In this chapter we will explore three sensory systems that play a more discrete role in the classroom but still influence regulation. It is easy to overlook the gustatory, olfactory, and interoceptive sensory systems when considering why a student may be behaving in a certain manner. In particular, the interoceptive system serves as an important foundation to understanding and detecting emotions. A student who cannot appropriately identify their emotions may not actually be feeling them internally—or may be feeling them too intensely. This can result in considerable dysregulation that makes the student more prone to meltdowns and irritability. Processing input from all three of these systems allows students to meet our most basic physiological needs— eating, drinking, using the bathroom—so that they can attend to, participate in, and engage with academic activities.

What are the Gustatory, Olfactory, and Interoceptive Systems?

Oral input *is a combination of what we taste, smell, and feel in our mouths.* This might include "the teacher's perfume or lotion, body odor from other peers, the woody taste of a recorder in music class, a peer's pickle sandwich at lunch, rubber balls in PE class, a mealy apple, or an air freshener in the bathroom."[1]

As you can see from the diagram, **gustatory input**, *or what we taste,* is received by the mouth and processed in the parietal lobe near the sensorimotor area. There are five different tastes: sweet, salty, sour, bitter, and umami (savory).[2] Most of what we eat has some combination of these tastes in one dish. Eating is a highly complex, stimulating sensory activity that we do on a very regular basis. The intensity of flavors and tastes can vary from one meal to the next, even when eating the same food. For example, an apple or pear or tomato can taste more sweet or more sour depending on its ripeness. The predictability of processed, packaged food is one reason students may prefer these items in their lunch—they know exactly what to expect every time they eat it.

As you can see from the diagram, **olfactory input**, *or what we smell,* is received by the nose and processed in the frontal lobe. Most of what we taste—80–90%—is actually due to our olfactory system through a mechanism called retronasal olfaction. **Retronasal olfaction**, or "mouth smelling", is *smell that enters the nose through the back of the mouth to enhance the taste of food and beverages.*[2,3] You have probably experienced a lack of this taste when you have congestion in your nose. What we smell is important for our safety: a burning smell tells us there is a fire, a rancid smell tells us something is spoiled, a fetid smell tells us we need to manage our personal hygiene. What we smell is also important for the emotion we experience with memories.[3] The warm, comforting smell of cinnamon when baking cookies with a loved one contrasted with the putrid, nauseating smell of garlic during the first trimester of pregnancy. A student may enjoy the smell of a new textbook because it reminds them of going to the bookstore on a weekly basis with their grandpa. Or another student may gag at the smell of tomato soup because they recall that smell from when they had a stomach bug. Interestingly, we tend to habituate quickly to familiar odors; but just because we do not smell them does not mean they are not influencing our state of regulation.[3] For example, synthetic odors (e.g., air fresheners and cleaning products) can have negative consequences with long-term exposure, such as headaches or nausea, without people even realizing it.[4]

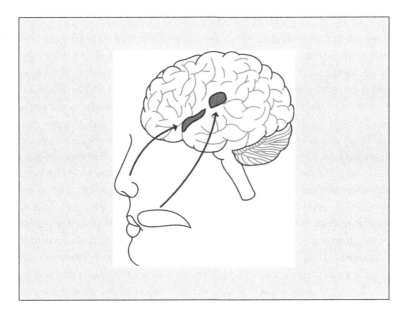

Figure 9.1 The Gustatory and Olfactory Systems

Sensory input for the gustatory (taste) system is received by the tongue and then transmitted to the gustatory cortex in the parietal lobe for processing. Sensory input for the olfactory (smell) system is received by the nose and then transmitted to the olfactory cortex in the frontal lobe for processing.

In addition to taste and smell, there is a large amount of tactile and proprioceptive input that is involved in putting something into our mouth. We need to know where the food is in our mouth in order to effectively chew and swallow it.[2] We need to know where our tongue is in our mouth so we don't bite down on it when we're chewing or talking. We need to know whether the texture in our mouth is safe to swallow. We need to know not to chew and swallow a small chicken bone when we feel it in our mouth.

As mentioned in Chapter 8, chewing or sucking on something activates the proprioceptive system via muscles and joints in the mouth. This, like other forms of proprioceptive input, can have a positive influence on one's state of regulation. This is why students (or adults) might bite on their fingernails or chew on their pen or suck on their shirt when they are anxious. According to research, chewing gum *prior* to taking a test may briefly enhance performance while chewing gum *during* a test can be distracting.[5]

As seen in the diagram, **interoception** *input, or our ability to detect our internal needs*, is received by the internal organs and processed in the insula deep within the cerebral cortex. Interoception at school includes "going to the bathroom, identifying hunger, knowing when to put on a sweater for recess, or taking a break in PE when overheated."[1] Interoception is often called the hidden sense, because it facilitates many things we don't do consciously such as recognizing signals of hunger, thirst, change in temperature, level of fatigue, and need to use the bathroom. We can also monitor our heart rate and breathing as a function of the interoceptive system. "Interoception allows us to detect that something is off and then address that need in the near future."[1] Students who struggle with interoceptive cues may seem like they are avoiding school work or making excuses or being demanding, when in reality they cannot accurately assess what their bodies need. Examples include asking to wear a sweatshirt in class even though the temperature seems comfortable, using the bathroom multiple times within a class period, expressing that they are "starving" even though they just ate a snack, or requiring constant reminders to drink water throughout the day.

The vagus nerve serves as the communication highway between the internal organs and the brain.[6] When we have physiological (body-based) needs that must be met, the vagus nerve sends signals to help those needs get met in order to keep the autonomic nervous system in balance. Responding to internal signals requires some level of attention; when our attention is shifted to another task or regaining a state of regulation then our internal

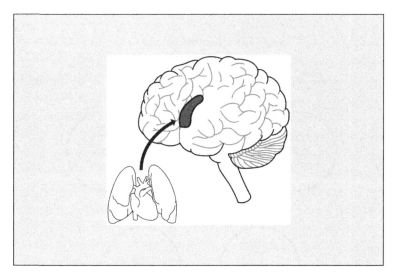

Figure 9.2 The Interoceptive System

Sensory input for the interoceptive system is received by the internal organs (heart, lungs, stomach, intestines, bladder) and then transmitted to the insula deep within the cerebral cortex for processing.

needs tend to go unmet. Think about a time when you were so engaged in an activity that you didn't realize you needed to use the bathroom until you stood up from that activity. Or think about a time when you were so upset about something that you didn't even realize how hungry you were until after your friend comforted you. Physical symptoms such as stomach aches, diarrhea, constipation, headaches, rapid heartbeat, or daytime wetting, can occur when interoceptive signals are altered as a result of heightened stress.[7]

Similarly, many of the physiological signals sent from internal organs reflect felt emotions.[6] This helps us to discern different emotions and identify how we feel in a particular moment. When we feel sad our heart "hurts", our breathing becomes shallower, our muscles get floppy, and our appetite may be lost. When we feel anxious our heart rate speeds up, our palms start sweating, our muscles get tense, and our stomach feels uneasy. These bodily cues from our internal organs give us additional clues about how we are feeling, allowing us to respond appropriately to our emotional needs. However, sometimes we confuse physiological signals with emotions, such as when we become "hangry"

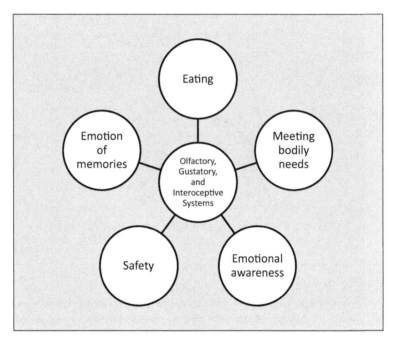

Figure 9.3 Supportive Diagram

The olfactory and gustatory systems contribute largely to the process of eating. Interoception is critical to responding to our internal body needs, like using the bathroom and detecting hunger and thirst. The diagram outlines the primary ways in which the olfactory, gustatory, and interoceptive systems impact us on a regular basis.

(hungry + angry). We may not realize that our increased irritability or frustration or annoyance is actually a result of being hungry. "Making sure students have all their interoceptive needs met is therefore very important for the process of learning and regulation."[1]

How do the Gustatory, Olfactory, and Interoceptive Systems Impact Regulation and Learning?

These three sensory systems play a more indirect role in learning but are highly influential on overall regulation. Taste and smell are critical to the process of eating. If a student is not eating enough or not eating nutritiously then this can negatively impact their arousal level, which may result in difficulty attending to the learning material. In Chapter 11 we dive deeper into the impact of diet on sensory processing and regulation.

As with Avi, if a student struggles with interoceptive processing then internal cues may be dysregulating and negatively impact attention in the classroom. They may appear distracted or disengaged when, in fact, they need to use the bathroom or put on a sweater or get a drink of water. Attending to these basic needs first will allow them to better listen to the teacher, organize their independent work time, or think clearly and creatively. Difficulty with interoceptive processing can also result in poor emotional awareness, resulting in poor self-awareness, difficulty relating to the emotions of peers, and frequent meltdowns. All of these will undoubtedly interfere with a student's ability to navigate peer relationships, establish a protective relationship with the teacher, and remain regulated enough to take on academic demands.

Here are several examples of common classroom activities that require a high degree of gustatory, olfactory, or interoceptive processing:

- *Using the bathroom*

  We rely on the interoceptive system to know when we need to urinate or have a bowel movement. And when we're in the process the interoceptive system helps us know that we've completely emptied the bladder or finished with a bowel movement … so we don't need to go again in 30 minutes.

  The bathroom also carries a lot of unique smells. A combination of urine and feces plus air fresheners and soap. This can be a lot for a little body to take in! Some students may not be bothered at all by these smells, some may actually like the strong odor of the air freshener, and some may need to plug their nose the entire time. Just keep this in mind the next time a student complains about using the bathroom at school.

- *Eating snack and lunch*

  As mentioned, eating is one of the most sensory stimulating activities in which we regularly engage: all of the tastes and smells, on top of the texture and temperature of foods, plus the coordination of the muscles to chew and swallow. Thus, it can be challenging for students to regulate themselves during snack time and lunch. Yet, ironically, eating is one of the ways in which students maintain appropriate glucose levels to stay engaged with learning.

Eating also requires the interoceptive system to know when to eat and how much to eat. This system helps to warn us that we are getting hungry in order to prevent the depletion of glucose and other essential nutrients. It also helps ensure we eat enough without overeating. Because the interoceptive system is closely tied to the brain's emotional center, when a student feels stressed, anxious, or sad they may not "feel" like eating or may only want to eat foods that make them "feel" good. When a student does not eat enough throughout the day the brain is not getting the nutrients it needs, resulting in difficulty with attending, learning, and engaging (remember the needs of the lower levels of the brain must be met before the higher levels can be fully accessed!).

- *Participating in art class*

You might not immediately think about art class when it comes to the olfactory system, but there is a wide variety of smells associated with art materials. Clay, paint, markers, charcoal crayons all have distinctive smells—some better than others. Staying regulated while taking in all these unique smells can be challenging for some students.

- *Participating in PE class*

PE class is another place where a wide variety of smells are involved. Rubber balls, sweaty students, a musky gym; the conspicuous odors hit you right away as you enter this space. You might find that a particular student does well in PE class when it's held outside where smells are more natural and diffused, but has more difficulty participating when it's held in a congested gymnasium.

The physical activity that occurs in PE class naturally increases the body's temperature, resulting in sweating and increased heart rate. Some students may feel uncomfortable with these internal signals, thus limiting the degree or intensity with which they participate in activities. Other students may not seem to know their limits and may require you to step in to suggest a break to prevent from overheating or overexhaustion. Additionally, prolonged movement activities may actually mask other internal cues, such as needing to use the bathroom. It may be that once the movement activity stops the student feels a sudden urgency to use the bathroom "now!" because they didn't register that need when running around.

We know that it may be difficult to determine, during the course of a busy day in a busy classroom, whether a student is overstimulated or understimulated with sensory input, or is having a difficult time discriminating sensory information. However, we want to provide you with some signs to look out for and behaviors to consider. Remember to be curious about why a student may be demonstrating different behaviors or presenting with challenges in their learning. If you have more questions you can certainly reach out to the occupational therapist on staff at your school.

Here we expand upon signs taken from our book *The "Why" Behind Classroom Behaviors: Integrative Strategies for Learning, Regulation, and Relationships,* in order to help you determine if there is a pattern of challenges that may indicate a sensory processing disorder. *Note: (G) denotes gustatory, (O) denotes olfactory, and (I) denotes interoceptive.*

When a student's gustatory, olfactory, and interoceptive systems are *understimulated* you may see the following:

- Loves spicy, sour, flavorful food (G)
- Makes noises constantly with mouth (G)
- Requests gum or peppermints (G)
- Smells objects frequently (O)
- Doesn't seem to notice strong-smelling odors (O)
- Needs to pee "right now!", even though five minutes earlier they tried and weren't successful (I)
- Doesn't notice hunger until "starving" (I)
- Requires constant reminders to drink water throughout the day (I)
- Body temperature runs hot (I)
- Doesn't stop until exhausted (I)

When a student's gustatory, olfactory, and interoceptive systems is *overstimulated* you may see the following:

- Limited food variety (G/O)
- Sensitive gag reflex (G/O)
- Refuses to eat around strong food smells, such as in the cafeteria (O)

- Comments about the smell of body odor or people's breath (O)
- Complains about being hot or cold on a regular basis (I)
- Feels heartbeat pounding (I)
- Urinates frequently throughout the day (I)
- Dislikes having a bowel movement (I)
- Poor tolerance for any sign of hunger (I)

When a student's gustatory, olfactory, and interoceptive systems cannot *discriminate* you may see the following:

- Bites tongue or cheek when chewing (G)
- Difficulty moving tongue (G)
- Overstuffs mouth (G)
- Poor ability to describe feel of food in mouth (G)
- Difficulty telling if something smells good or bad (O)
- Difficulty knowing when to use the restroom (I)
- Needs reminders to eat or drink throughout the day (I)
- Eats too much or too little at meals (I)
- Confuses emotions with internal needs, such as feeling sad when they are actually hungry (I)
- Confuses internal needs with emotions, such as feeling nauseous when they are actually anxious (I)

Experience It!—Poor Oral Discrimination

Purchase kalamata olives with and without pits, or grapes with and without seeds. Put several of each in a bowl. Close your eyes and eat one of them. Repeat this several times until you've eaten some with and without the pits/seeds.

Reflect on the following questions afterwards:

1) Were you nervous at all about possibly swallowing a pit or a seed?

2) How quickly were you able to discern if the olive or grape had a seed?

3) Did you change the way you ate the olive or grape when it had a pit/seed compared to when it was pitless/seedless?

4) How might this impact your ability to socially engage when eating?

This activity is designed to help you better understand what a student with poor oral discrimination might experience when eating. The child might rely heavily on what a food looks like—only wanting to eat what is familiar and wanting to see the packaging of the food—in order to ensure their safety so they don't choke. It may be completely dysregulating (and possibly unsafe) if a child picked up a grape expecting it to be seedless but found it to have a seed. They may stop eating grapes all together as an adaptive strategy. And they certainly aren't focused on the conversations around the table!

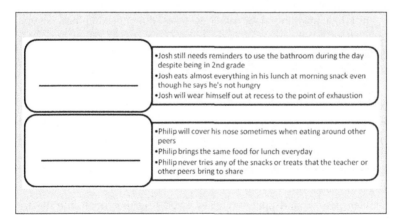

- Josh still needs reminders to use the bathroom during the day despite being in 2nd grade
- Josh eats almost everything in his lunch at morning snack even though he says he's not hungry
- Josh will wear himself out at recess to the point of exhaustion

- Philip will cover his nose sometimes when eating around other peers
- Philip brings the same food for lunch everyday
- Philip never tries any of the snacks or treats that the teacher or other peers bring to share

Figure 9.4 Interactive Scenario

Read the stories about students that describe *patterns* the teacher has observed over several months. Determine if the student is experiencing difficulty with olfactory/gustatory/interoceptive understimulation, overstimulation, or discrimination.

Sensory-Smart Gustatory, Olfactory, and Interoceptive Strategies for Every Classroom

After determining a particular student's response to gustatory, olfactory, and interoceptivel input, it's important to have some strategies in your back pocket to help support those needs. As teachers, we know you have so much to consider and so many students to support. Remember that you can always reach out to the school occupational therapist for more help; these strategies are not meant to replace additional therapy. However, implementing some of these strategies can help the overall regulation and learning of the majority of students in your class. Through attending to your nonverbal cues, monitoring your tone of voice, and maintaining a calm presence with your students you will send them a message of safety and comfort while also supporting their sensory needs.[1] Looking at the opening vignette, Ms. Olsen, who was already taking an approach of curiosity, might say to Avi, "It seems like you always need to go to the bathroom a lot during my class. I want you to take care of your body but I also want to make sure you're completing your work and students are not becoming distracted. Let's come up with a plan that seems fair to both of us."

Just like anything new, progress takes time; making new neural connections takes time. Give each strategy a few weeks to see how your students respond and adapt to the changes you make, then reassess what may need to be adjusted. There may be a combination of strategies that a student may need, which often requires a trial and error process.[1] Try not to get discouraged if only small changes are seen; these are important neurological stepping stones towards a larger goal. Ms. Olsen may start by allowing Avi to sit closest to the door so he can more readily access the bathroom without disrupting other students. They could also develop a subtle signal that Avi gives to Ms. Olsen to indicate that he needs to leave to use the bathroom.

Here we expand upon strategies taken from our book *The "Why" Behind Classroom Behaviors: Integrative Strategies for Learning, Regulation, and Relationships,* in order to support students with their gustatory, olfactory, or interoceptive processing.

To promote appropriate gustatory, olfactory, and interoceptive processing *for all students:*

- When using essential oils in the class remember that scents like lavender, rose, chamomile, eucalyptus, and jasmine are calming. Cinnamon, orange, peppermint, and rosemary tend to be more alerting and energizing (O)
- Allow students to access water bottles and snacks throughout the day, particularly during independent work time. Many students find that chewing on something or sucking something through a straw is helpful to maintain focus (G)
- Avoid wearing strong-smelling perfume or cologne (O)
- Do not use synthetic air fresheners or deodorizing sprays and limit strong-smelling disinfectants or cleaners (O)
- Try to brush your teeth after eating or drinking, such as in the morning after coffee or during the day after lunch (O)
- Do not dismiss (or use it as an incentive!) when a student is communicating a bodily need, even if you feel they are using it as "an escape." Many emotions can cause physiological reactions—such as needing to urinate when nervous—so it is important to explore "why" a student is repeatedly requesting a bodily need be met (I)
- Talk about different signals that our bodies might give to let us know when we are thirsty (dry mouth, sore throat, headache, sweating), hungry (stomach pain, grumbling sound), tired (sweating, body slouching, heart beating fast or slow, eyes drooping), or need to use the bathroom (bladder pain, leg shaking) (I)
- Integrate yoga into the class with a focus on deep breathing, feeling changes in heart rate, and checking in with the body (I)

To provide *more* gustatory, olfactory, or interoceptive input for *understimulation:*

- ARK Therapeutic makes a wide variety of "chewlery" and pencil toppers that students can use for oral input (G)

- Crunchy snacks provide tactile input to the mouth which can be alerting, especially during independent work time. We typically recommend: trail mix, popcorn, pretzels, carrots, celery, or apples (G)

- Mints and cinnamon candies are very alerting, which can help students better focus (G)

- Allow the student to have a cold water bottle with a straw at his desk (G)

- Allow the student to use scented markers or crayons (O)

- Encourage the student to wear a vibrating watch that notifies when to urinate, drink water, and/or have a snack (I)

- Have the student take breaks every hour to check in with their body regarding internal cues (I)

- Allow frequent movement breaks to encourage a change in position (I)

To provide *less* gustatory, olfactory, or interoceptive input for *overstimulation:*

- Chewy snacks (including gum) provide proprioceptive input to the mouth which can be calming, especially during independent work time. We typically recommend: fruit leather, dried fruit, beef jerky, or bagels (G)

- Dry erase markers have strong odors, whereas chalk, dry erase crayons, and SMART Boards are low odor (O)

- Be conscious of the amount of hairspray, perfume, cologne, or lotion that you wear (O)

- Be conscious of the odors associated with a class pet (O)

- Remove air fresheners and refrain from using spray air fresheners (O)

- Move the garbage can away from student desks (O)

- Use a garbage can with a lid (O)

- Have the student take three deep breaths with his hand placed over his heart when feeling overwhelmed with a body signal (I)

- Allow the student access to water and snacks throughout the day (I)

- Grant access to the bathroom no matter how frequently it is requested (I)

To help support a student's difficulty with gustatory, olfactory, or interoceptive *discrimination:*

- ARK Therapeutic makes a wide variety of "chewlery" and pencil toppers that children can use for oral input (G)
- Ask the student to describe the taste or smell of something and compare that to a more familiar taste or smell (G/O)
- Have the student take three deep breaths before determining if something is an internal body signal versus an emotion (I)
- Provide a visual representation of different emotions and how those may be reflected in body signals (I)
- Encourage the student to wear a vibrating watch that notifies when to urinate, drink water, and/or have a snack (I)
- Have the student take breaks every hour to check in with their body regarding internal cues (I)

Special Accommodations at Lunch and Snack Time to Consider for Children with Oral-based Challenges

- Allow the student to sit at a table with a smaller group of classmates
- Allow the student to change where they are sitting if another classmate has something they don't like to smell
- Allow the student to sit close to an open window or open door to allow some of the smell to dissipate
- Allow the student to sit away from the lunch counter and away from the garbage cans
- Ask the parent to send a box of preferred snacks so when other students share a treat the student still has something special to eat

Reflective Activity

Ways I already support the olfactory, gustatory, and interoceptive systems of my students	• •
New ways that I can support the olfactory, gustatory, and interoceptive systems of my students	• •
Students who may need additional oral-based or interoceptive-based support	• •
Ways I notice that I process olfactory, gustatory, and interoceptive input	• •

Now that you know more about the olfactory, gustatory, and olfactory systems and their impact on learning and regulation, think about how you can apply this information to your classroom.

References

1. Chaves, J., & Taylor, A. (2020). *The "Why" behind Classroom Behaviors: Integrated Strategies for Learning, Regulation, and Relationships*. Thousand Oaks, CA: Corwin.

2. Stuckey, B. (2012). *Taste What You're Missing: The Passionate Eater's Guide to Why Food Tastes Good*. New York: Atria Books.

3. Rosenblum, L. (2011). *See What I'm Saying: The Extraordinary Powers of Our Five Senses*. New York: W. W. Norton & Co.

4. Steinemann, A. (2016). Fragranced consumer products: Exposures and effects from emissions. *Air Quality, Atmosphere & Health*, 9(8), 861–866.

5. Onyper, S. V., Carr, T. L, Farrar, J. S., & Floyd, B. R. (2011). Cognitive advantages of chewing gum: Now you see them, now you don't. *Appetite, 57*(2), 321–328.

6. Mayer, E. (2016). *The Mind-Gut Connection: How the Hidden Conversation within Our Bodies Impacts Our Mood, Our Choices, and Our Overall Health.* New York: Harper Wave.

7. Schulz, A., & Vogle, C. (2015). Interoception and stress. *Frontiers in Psychology, 6*, 993.

10 | Postural Stability and Praxis

It was Tuesday. PE class was on Tuesdays. Dani trudged slowly into school that morning. Ms. Ravine also knew it was going to be another challenging day. This was the third week of learning dance steps in PE. The previously two weeks resulted in Dani falling to the floor intentionally, goofing off in front of peers, or intentionally messing up. Ms. Ravine didn't understand why Dani acted this way, especially because her other teachers raved about how well Dani did in their classes. Yes, learning dance steps was hard for some students; Ms. Ravine could admit that. Yet every other student seemed to have grasped the steps by now and at least seemed to *try*.

Today Ms. Ravine entered the gymnasium in a heightened state of arousal, as did Dani. They both dreaded this time of day because it was exhausting for both of them. After only ten minutes into the class, Dani had already thrown herself onto the floor and started moaning loudly. Nothing Ms. Ravine said seemed to help Dani stand up again, and Ms. Ravine lost her patience. "Dani. You need to stand up and try harder. You can do this, you just need to focus." Dani, however, just started to cry. "My body is broken," Dani said. "I just want to go home."

What Ms. Ravine didn't know is that Dani also struggled with coordination-based activities at recess as well. She often sat out when several of her friends wanted to play jump rope. Dani seemed to intentionally mess up when playing hand-clapping games with her friends, resulting in peers getting frustrated with her or refusing to play with her. Sometimes Dani would just play by herself because it was easier than dealing with the ridicule associated with playing with her friends.

Dani's difficulty with participating in dance class, jump rope, and hand-clapping games all stemmed from dyspraxia. **Dyspraxia** *is, essentially, difficulty with motor coordination.* Because dyspraxia can look very different in each child, and because it can be a subtle underlying factor to other learning challenges, it is often left misdiagnosed or undiagnosed until a later age. Yet children who struggle with dyspraxia can feel trapped in their bodies—their mind is telling their body what to do but their body just won't cooperate. It can lead to goofing off behaviors, like with Dani, as a means to cope with the frustration they feel.

What are Postural Stability and Praxis?

Postural stability and praxis are integral to how we support our bodies and move our bodies efficiently. This may include sitting upright in a chair, climbing the ladder on the playground, imitating a dance move in PE class, or opening a container at lunch.

Postural stability *is the co-contraction between muscles in the front of our body (flexors) and back of our body (extensors) to hold a steady position.* It is also the ability to resist gravity—while still remaining balanced—when our body is moved in different directions. Postural stability serves as our foundation of support. "We must have adequate proximal (i.e., close to the body) stability in order to manipulate objects away from our body."[1] Without proper postural stability and postural responses, a student may focus so much of his attention on maintaining a stable position in the chair that they cannot attend to the lesson plan or write efficiently or solve a complex math problem.[3] Students do this subtly as they reach out in front of them to pick up a book or move their arm across the paper to write. They do this more noticeably as they lean down to grab a book out of their backpack or turn their head to talk to a peer.

Postural stability establishes confidence in our ability to move our body without falling over—to trust that we can move our body parts separately while still remaining stable. This requires **equilibrium responses**, *whereby our head, arms, legs, hips, and trunk compensate when our center of gravity is shifted.* If equilibrium responses are delayed or inadequate then this can result in difficulty with regaining postural control, often causing balance or realignment back to a centered position to be disrupted.[2] Postural instability can lead to fear of movement on unstable surfaces, fear of swings and slides, fear of having one's feet off the ground, or fear of someone else moving their body because they cannot trust that their body will make the appropriate adjustments to remain in a stable, upright position.

Sitting in an upright position, through the use of postural responses, is ergonomically important as well. This helps with the alignment of the head, neck, and back in order to maximize strength and stability, as well as prevent chronic pain and soreness. Students with poor postural stability may tend to forward flex at the neck, which can result in long-term implications for the shoulders, neck, and back, as well as make the eyes work harder to focus.

Praxis *is the ability to ideate, motor plan, and execute a motor action.* Praxis requires a high degree of cognitive engagement and attention, although this becomes more automatic as skills are acquired.[3] Ideation praxis allows us to formulate an idea around what an object might do.

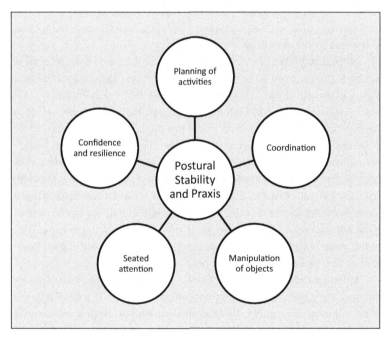

Figure 10.1 Supportive Diagram

Praxis and postural stability largely influence the quality and efficiency of our movements. The diagram outlines the primary ways in which praxis and postural stability impact us on a regular basis.

154

Motor planning allows us to formulate a plan around how to move our body to make an object do something. Execution praxis allows us to appropriately execute the plan of how to move our body. In particular, we rely on our praxic abilities in *novel* situations. We draw on past experiences to inform our ideas, plans, and movements around new experiences. Once these situations and experiences become routine or have been repeated enough times we form "motor memory" around them and they become more automatic.[3] We can then start to generalize these movement patterns for new experiences and in new environments.

Postural stability and praxis require the integration of our tactile, proprioceptive, and vestibular systems. The complex relationship between these systems allows us to rely on our **body map**—or the *relationship of one body part to another*—in order to perform movements and adjust our body position. Essentially, we can "do without thinking".[3] This frees up the brain to engage in other more cognitively demanding activities while we are executing postural stability or engaged in tasks that require praxis— precisely what students are required to do on a regular basis at school.

How do Postural Stability and Praxis Impact Regulation and Learning?

Before postural stability and praxis can be addressed, a student must have well-established processing of the vestibular, proprioceptive, and tactile sensory systems. The integration of these three sensory systems results in these two sensory-based motor skills. Postural stability sets the stage for one's sense of security in moving one's body. It is nearly impossible to focus on learning a new concept in the classroom if one does not feel competent in adjusting one's body position. Appropriate praxis skills provide meaning to one's actions and interactions. Praxis serves as the foundation for the organization of one's behavior and ability to engage in higher level cognitive processes, such as those required in a school setting. The conceptualization of ideas and movements within the body help to inform the conceptualization of ideas outside of the body.[2] The feedback loop involved in praxis also allows for us to evaluate and reflect on the movement experience in order to learn from it and perform it more efficiently in the future—another important factor for academic engagement.[3]

Students with dyspraxia may have acquired **splinter skills**—*or the ability to do a specific task that does not generalize to another task*—but acquiring new skills takes considerable time and effort.[3] When an activity is changed, even slightly, a student with dyspraxia may have difficulty being successful; conditions must be perfect. Yes, practicing a new skill over and over again until mastery occurs is possible, but also exhausting and oftentimes frustrating.[4] This is true even for tasks that seem routine. Students with dyspraxia may appear awkward when completing a motor activity because they are working hard to compensate. "Frequently students with praxis difficulties are reported to be 'uncoordinated', 'lazy', taught basic things that seem to come naturally to others, take a long time to take decisions ('he can never decide what he wants'), perform tasks inconsistently ('she can do it but most of the time she wants me to do it'), and/or throw tantrums or get frustrated easily."[1]

If you see a student who is getting frustrated easily, completing tasks quickly, anxious about moving their body, fearful of new experiences, or has low self-esteem, take a moment to dig a little deeper and ask why the student is experiencing this dysregulation. There may be an underlying sensory-based motor disorder that impacts the student's postural stability or praxis and interferes with his ability to focus on learning. A student with dyspraxia may be avoidant, controlling, or a perfectionist in order to preserve their regulation because they do not want to experience failure yet again.[1]

Here are some common classroom activities that require a high degree of postural stability and praxis:

- *Sitting upright*

  As noted in previous chapters, sitting requires a high degree of vestibular and proprioceptive processing. Postural stability is a result of the dynamic interplay between these two sensory systems. Put simply, the vestibular system must be conveying information about gravity and muscle tone while the proprioceptive system must be conveying information about when and how much to contract certain muscles. As previously mentioned, when students sit upright in a chair or on the rug, the muscles in the front of the body—the flexors—must be in balance with the muscles in the back of the body—the extensors—in order to maintain a stable position. Additionally, slight adjustments that need to occur in our posture, like when the head is moved or the arm is moved, require equilibrium responses in order to not fall over or shift around dramatically. If a student must focus on co-contraction or equilibrium responses, they may become easily fatigued or prefer to lie down, slouch, or lean against something as a means to compensate. Appendix D has a variety of supportive seating options that may be appropriate for a student who demonstrates difficulty sitting upright.

- *Writing*

  Postural stability is foundational when it comes to writing. The proximal stability gained through the co-contraction of our muscles allows us to be in an upright position that supports the mobility of our shoulder, wrist, and fingers when moving the pencil across the paper. Additionally, as we move our arm across the paper, our body must make slight adjustments to posture in order to remain centered. If a student experiences postural instability his focus may shift to remaining stable, resulting in a compromise in legibility of handwriting or depth of thought.

  In order to appropriately manipulate the pencil and form each individual letter and number, praxis is required. Mature manipulation of the pencil necessitates the fingers move separately from the hand and shoulder in order to efficiently form letters and numbers. Every letter and number has a unique motor pattern associated with it, which requires motor planning in order to learn. Praxis continues to be important in order for these letter and number patterns to become automatic—forming them without much thought or effort.

- *Organization of ideas and materials*

  Students use ideation praxis and motor planning often when organizing their desks, backpacks, and lockers. Ideation praxis plays a large role in sequencing tasks, following multi-step directions, and creating a linear story. Getting organized to start a large project or managing multiple homework assignments also requires a large degree of planning associated with ideation praxis. A student who struggles with praxis may need additional scaffolding to keep their workspace neat, such as a picture reference of what their desk should look like; carry out multi-step tasks, such as a written reminder of each step; or keep track of homework assignments, such as color-coding folders for each class.

- *Participating in PE class*

    The need for postural stability and praxis might be most evident during PE class. With students running around, approaching from behind, or being accidentally bumped during different games, the ability to adjust one's posture and remain in a stable position is crucial.

    Often PE class introduces new games, activities, or dance steps to students, which requires appropriate praxis. Students must draw on previous motor experiences to successfully ideate what to do, motor plan how to efficiently do it, and then coordinate their bodies to execute the plan. Due to the fast-paced nature of many PE games, this must happen quickly or the student will get left behind. Most students may only need a few repetitions while other students may require several days of practice or more pointed modeling from the teacher. Students with dyspraxia may execute coordination-based activities, like dancing or jumping jacks or jumping rope, as quickly as possible because this compensates for performing controlled movements.

- *Playing at recess*

    Much like PE class, playing at recess requires a large degree of postural stability and praxis. Riding a tricycle, going down a slide, sitting on a swing, balancing on curbs, all require postural stability in order to successfully remain in an upright posture without falling. Students often play games that require close contact with one another at recess, which means accidentally pushing each other or "sneak attacking" each other. For students with poor postural stability they may opt to play alone because these types of games evoke anxiety that they may fall down because they cannot adequately retain or regain their stability.

    Climbing, playing hopscotch, jumping rope, sports games, all require appropriate praxis in order to participate. Students are always changing up games to keep them exciting and stimulating, so learning new rules and motor aspects of these games also requires ideation and motor planning. Students who struggle with praxis may opt to play the same game repeatedly, request to direct the play, or choose to play alone in order to compensate for difficulty with the coordination required during certain activities.

We know that it may be difficult to determine, during the course of a busy day in a busy classroom, whether a student is struggling with postural stability or praxis. However, we want to provide you with some signs to look out for and behaviors to consider. The important thing is that you are being curious about why a student may be demonstrating different behaviors or presenting with challenges in their learning. If you have more questions you can certainly reach out to the occupational therapist on staff at your school.

Here we expand upon signs taken from our book *The "Why" Behind Classroom Behaviors: Integrative Strategies for Learning, Regulation, and Relationships,* in order to help you determine if there is a pattern of challenges that may indicate a sensory processing disorder.

When a student is struggling with *postural stability* you may see the following:

- Difficulty sitting up in a chair or during circle time
- Fatigues easily with school work
- Slumps, slouches, or hunches over work when sitting
- Complains about writing and reading activities
- Sits with legs in a "W" position (a.k.a. W-sitting)
- Expresses fear of climbing, swinging, and riding bicycles at recess or PE
- Moves around frequently when standing in line
- Difficulty standing still when talking

When a student is struggling with *praxis* you may see the following:

- Seems unsure about how to perform a new task
- Prefers to do the same activities over and over, such as at recess
- Avoids learning new activities, particularly those requiring coordination
- Expresses frustration during sports-related activities
- Appears clumsy and uncoordinated
- Has difficulty using scissors
- Performs activities and movements in an inefficient manner
- Has a difficult time navigating the classroom

- Resists writing activities
- Demonstrates poor frustration tolerance, low self-esteem, and/or resilience
- Has a difficult time organizing their space
- Has a difficult time communicating what they want to do
- Takes a long time to initiate an activity
- Struggles with multi-step directions
- Requires assistance to manage buttons, snaps, or zippers on clothes

Experience It!—Dyspraxia

Look up different ways to tie a shoelace online. There are three ways people tend to tie their shoelaces: 1) Around the Tree method, 2) Bunny Ears method, and 3) Ian method. Identify which way you typically tie your shoelaces, then time yourself tying it this way while you're saying aloud what you did earlier in the day. Pick one of the other methods, practice two or three times, then time yourself tying it this way while you're saying aloud what you will do tomorrow.

Reflect on the following questions afterwards:

1) What was the time difference between the two methods?

2) How much more effort was required for the second method compared to the method you typically use?

3) What are other activities that would be challenging if you had to approach them a different way each time? (Examples: folding laundry, putting on a shirt, getting into your car)

This activity is designed to help you better understand what a student with dyspraxia might experience. Even simple activities, like tying a shoelace, can be difficult and frustrating for this student—and require a high level of focus, almost like they have to relearn the task each time. As you can imagine, this can be quite exhausting! This is compounded when the student must complete another motor planning task—talking—on top of tying their shoe.

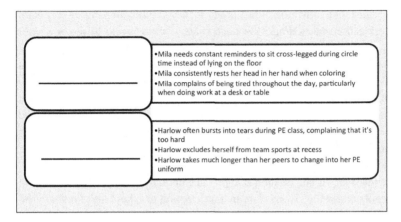

Figure 10.2 Interactive Scenario

Read the stories about students that describe *patterns* the teacher has observed over several months. Determine if the student is experiencing difficulty with postural stability or praxis.

Sensory-Smart Praxis and Postural Stability Strategies for Every Classroom

After determining a particular student's postural stability and praxis abilities, it's important to have some strategies in your back pocket to help support those needs. As teachers, we know you have so much to consider and so many students to support. Remember that you can always reach out to the school occupational therapist for more help; these strategies are not meant to replace additional therapy. However, implementing some of these strategies can help the overall regulation and learning of the majority of students in your class. Through attending to your nonverbal cues, monitoring your tone of voice, and maintaining a calm presence with your students you will send them a message of safety and comfort while also supporting their sensory needs.[1] On the day of dance class, Ms. Ravine might observe, "These dance steps can be tricky to learn, Dani. I know you're trying your hardest. Why don't you help me with the music today instead? We can work on the dance steps another time."

Just like anything new, progress takes time; making new neural connections takes time. Give each strategy a few weeks to see how your students respond and adapt to the changes you make, then reassess what may need to be adjusted. There may be a combination of strategies that a student may need, which often requires a trial and error process.[1] Try not to get discouraged if only small changes are seen; these are important neurological stepping stones towards a larger goal. Ms. Ravine could send home the pictures of the dance steps with Dani for her to work on with her parents. The next week during dance class Dani may be able to participate in the first ten minutes of class before she gets frustrated and falls to the floor. As she continues to practice her dance steps at home and feel regulated during dance class by participating in other ways (like controlling the music), Dani's capacity to take on challenges increases and she can soon dance for twenty minutes before becoming dysregulated. Dani also starts to volunteer when Ms. Ravine asks students to demonstrate previously learned dance steps in front of the class. It is clear that, while dance is still quite challenging for Dani, she is certainly making progress.

Here we expand upon strategies taken from our book *The "Why" Behind Classroom Behaviors: Integrative Strategies for Learning, Regulation, and Relationships,* in order to support students with their postural stability and praxis skills.

To promote appropriate postural stability and praxis *for all students*:

- Allow students to choose alternative seating options when appropriate
- Make sure the student's feet are planted flat on the floor
- Use modeling and examples when explaining concepts
- Make activities fun, personalized, and motivating
- Acknowledge when a student is being successful, and help that student recognize their own strengths
- Keep your classroom clearly organized and labeled, and encourage your students to organize their desks, backpacks, cubbies, etc.

To help support a student's difficulty with *postural stability:*

- Provide more supportive seating options for desk work and circle time (e.g., ball chair, chair with arms, or bean bag chair)

- Do vestibular-based activities (jumping, yoga, neck stretches) before sitting down for desk work
- Allow frequent movement breaks
- Have the student lie on the ground on his stomach with a 3-inch binder when doing independent work
- Know the limits of the student and be OK with taking breaks

To help support a student's difficulty with *praxis:*

- Do "heavy work" activities (pushing, pulling, jumping) before sitting down for desk work
- Provide a visual schedule for each activity
- Break down activities into their component parts
- Ask the student to repeat the instructions of various steps that need to be completed
- Ask the student to describe how a new activity may be similar or different to a familiar activity
- Provide the student choices whenever possible; this gives him more control which will increase his willingness to participate
- Make a map or drawing of a plan before executing
- Take a picture of an organized desk, cubby, or locker for the student to use as a reference
- Give the student manipulatives to design a plan before executing
- Model what you want done in addition to providing verbal cues
- Encourage the student to consider a new way of using a familiar object
- Encourage the student to consider a new way of doing a familiar task
- Know the limits of the student and be OK with taking breaks
- Be patient and understanding!

Special Accommodations in PE to Consider for Children with Postural Stability and Praxis Challenges

- Send home exercises with the student a week in advance so they can practice them ahead of time

- Break down exercises into smaller component parts and anticipate that more practice will be necessary

- Ask the student to repeat instructions and rules to check for understanding

- Give the student more of a leadership role, such as being the referee, during whole-group activities (soccer, basketball, kickball, hockey) so they don't get lost in the mix

- Have the student stand in front of a mirror when learning new exercises

- Use a metronome during coordination-based activities to assist with timing

- Give the student options as to which activity they can complete

- Allow the student to take more frequent breaks

- Engage the entire class in yoga poses or cross-body (a.k.a. midline crossing) activities: touch right elbow to left knee then left elbow to right knee; draw a large infinity sign in the air; rotate at the waist with arms out to the side like a helicopter

- Engage the entire class in the "superman" position (lie on the floor on your tummy with arms straight in front and legs straight in back; lift head, arms, and legs off the floor like you're flying and hold that position for as long as possible)

- Engage the entire class in the "silly bug" position (lie on the floor on your back with arms crossed over your chest and knees bent; lift head and feet off the floor similar to doing a crunch; hold that position for as long as possible)

Reflective Activity

Ways I already support postural stability and praxis of my students	• •
New ways that I can support postural stability and praxis of my students	• •
Students who may need additional support with postural stability or praxis	• •

Now that you know more about postural stability and praxis and their impact on learning and regulation, think about how you can apply this information to your classroom.

References

1. Chaves, J., & Taylor, A. (2020). *The "Why" behind Classroom Behaviors: Integrated Strategies for Learning, Regulation, and Relationships.* Thousand Oaks, CA: Corwin.

2. Burpee, J. (2015). *Sensory Integrative Intensive* continuing education course. Medfield, MA: Educational Resources, Inc.

3. Ayers, A. J. (2005). *Sensory Integration and the Child: Understanding Hidden Sensory Challenges.* Los Angeles, CA: Western Psychological Services.

4. Case-Smith, J., Allen, A. S., & Pratt, P. N. (2001). *Occupational Therapy for Children* (6th ed.). St. Louis, MO: Mosby.

11 | How Sleep, Diet, and Screen Time Can Influence Sensory Processing and Regulation

While there are many things inside the classroom that you as teachers can influence in order to facilitate improved learning, there are also many things that you have no control over. The following are all variables that are difficult for teachers to influence directly within the classroom, but contribute to the teacher asking "why?" a certain behavior is happening. Knowledge of these variables may help to open up a conversation with caregivers in order to optimize the learning experience. Talking with students about the influence of these variables can be empowering as well. It is also important, as a teacher, for you to consider how your sleep patterns, diet, and screen time habits impact the way in which you co-regulate with students.

We recognize that all families do things differently. Every culture—and every household—has certain traditions, expectations, and ways of doing that will shape how a child develops and how a child is influenced by all of these external variables. We are not suggesting that there is a "right" or "wrong" way to navigate these areas. However, we do want to present what the research shows in order to help keep you better informed, help you approach students with empathy and understanding, and help guide discussions with caregivers.

There are also social justice concerns that may influence a student's sleep, diet, and use of screen time, including noise pollution, neighborhood violence, poor access to fruits and vegetables (e.g., food deserts), cost of healthy food, family work schedules, and unsafe outdoor play spaces, to name a few. You may also experience some of these social justice concerns yourself. Be aware that systemic racism may impact access to resources, interventions, and supports that students need.

Influence of Sleep

Sleep plays a critical role in maintaining balance in our body: restoration of brain cells, supporting brain plasticity, resting muscles and joints, and regulating our inner clock (i.e., circadian rhythm). According to the American Academy of Sleep Medicine, children 3–5 years old typically require at least ten hours of sleep, while children 6–12 years old typically require at least nine hours of sleep.[1] Poor sleep negatively impacts almost every area of brain-body functioning and development. It creates stress not only for the child but also for those surrounding the child. Many symptoms of sleep-deprived children look like difficulty processing sensory input.

Consider a student who chronically sleeps poorly. Their tiredness may manifest by constantly jumping or skipping around in an attempt to stay awake. They may frequently "zone out" or daydream during class, and they may chew on their sweatshirt or nails to help focus on a task. They might be more reactive towards peers, and their frustration tolerance might be limited or they might give up easily. For this student, spinning in a circle could be alerting. Any stimulating sensory strategy to say "wake up, body!" is likely. Anything that tests an already short fuse of a student who is chronically sleeping poorly will lead to a "zero to sixty" response. This is not a behavior problem that deserves punishment, but rather a cry for help to regulate and get back into a state of balance. Until the student receives the amount of sleep their body requires this cycle of dysregulation will continue to occur. As a teacher, when you don't sleep well or are consistently not getting enough sleep, you may notice that you become easily irritable, feel more antsy when focusing on a lesson plan, or get increasingly agitated with students talking or touching your body.

Concomitantly, many children with SPD have difficulty regulating themselves when it is time to sleep.[2] Sometimes the routine leading up to bedtime is stressful, hurried, and dysregulating, which impacts the quality of sleep. Sometimes the child is so overstimulated from the day that they can't settle to sleep. Or maybe the overstimulation from the day is so exhausting that the child wants to nap after school; then later that night they wake at 11pm and can't fall back asleep. At other times the events of the day are so understimulating that the child's body remains essentially in sleep mode all day long. And sometimes a child simply wakes up dysregulated from a restless night of sleep or because of other stressors in the home.

Sleep is essentially an exercise in self-regulation. However, many children with SPD have a difficult time self-regulating because they do not yet have the strategies to do so. Therefore co-regulation with a caregiver, changing the sleep environment, and use of external sensory inputs surrounding the sleep process will be necessary to keep a child regulated in order to fall asleep.

Some sensory-based strategies caregivers can use to facilitate improved sleep include:

- Visual
  - Use a nightlight
  - Use a star projector nightlight
  - Watch an LED fishtank toy
  - Use blackout curtains
  - Face the bed away from the window
  - Use a sleep mask

- Auditory
  - Use a sound machine
  - Play calming music
  - Wear noise-cancelling headphones
  - Utilize the iLs DreamPad

- Vestibular
  - Read books in a rocking chair
  - Sing songs in a rocking chair
  - Do yoga before bed

- Tactile
  - Use lycra sheets
  - Use a weighted blanket (research suggests 7–10% of child's body weight)
  - Wear an oversized t-shirt
  - Sleep naked

- Take a bath instead of a shower
- Shower or bathe in the morning instead of at night
- Proprioceptive
  - Use a weighted blanket (research suggests 7–10% of child's body weight)
  - Move the bed to a corner
  - Sleep under or on top of a bean bag
  - Use a body pillow
  - Provide a body massage while reading books
- Oral-Motor
  - Provide crunchy or chewy snacks
  - Use a chew tool when reading books
  - Keep a cup of water next to the bed
  - Use an electric toothbrush

While all children are different in their sleep routine preferences, there are a few things we regularly recommend. You can share these ideas with caregivers. Reassure caregivers that change is hard, so it may be met with initial resistance. Encourage caregivers to involve their child as much as possible in making decisions about bedtime.

- Stop screen time two to three hours before bedtime. Screen time can interfere with the ability to fall asleep.[3]
- Eat dinner early—about 2½ hours before bedtime. This will allow for digestion.
- Play hard for 30–45 minutes, about 1½ hours before you start the quiet bedtime routine.
- Transition to the calming routine by dimming the lights and playing classical instrumental music.
- Brush teeth before doing any other bedtime activity. This is usually not a favorite for most kids, so doing it first will allow for the other activities to reregulate them.

- Take a warm bath with lavender oil. Showers can be very stimulating because each stream can feel like a pin prick.

- Read two to three books, sing two or three songs, then turn the lights off.

You may find that some of these sensory strategies and routines are also helpful for you to increase the quality and quantity of your sleep so that you are in a more regulated state that allows you to better co-regulate with students. In fact, the American Academy of Sleep Medicine recommends seven to nine hours of sleep every night to promote optimal health in adults.[4]

Influence of Diet

What, how much, and how often a child eats on a regular basis also influences his state of regulation. This can vary dramatically from one student to the next. Some students may be more sensitive to certain foods, like gluten, or casein, or red dye, while others seem to have no problem eating anything placed in front of them. Some students may need to eat smaller amounts more frequently throughout the day in order to help restore their brain cells and keep their glucose levels up. This is often true in the morning and after cognitively challenging activities.

When we get hungry, particularly overly hungry, this negatively impacts regulation. Some students are more sensitive to this than others. Hunger (and thirst) can manifest in difficulty focusing, fidgeting behaviors, irritability, and decreased energy—all of which impede learning. As hunger takes over, our senses begin to heighten around finding food in order to sustain most basic needs (recall the vertical organization of the brain from Chapter 1). Because dysregulation starts to occur, sensory input that may typically not be bothersome starts to become annoying, frustrating, more noticeable, and distracting. This may look like an SPD because the student is doing whatever they can to stay regulated despite feeling hungry. However, once they eat a snack or lunch these behaviors disappear; they can again successfully participate in the learning process. Make sure that you, too, are eating enough so that you can stay in a regulated state during the school day. Take the time to eat breakfast in the morning (coffee doesn't count!), bring several quick snacks that you can eat throughout the day, and pack a nutritionally balanced lunch. Despite the oft-hurried and overscheduled nature of the school day, try to make this a priority. Remember, the needs of the lower levels of the brain must be met before you can fully access the higher levels of the brain required for engaging with students, delivering the lesson plan, and creatively problem solving unforeseen circumstances.

Students with an SPD may have a difficult time organizing themselves to eat, despite the fact that eating may actually be what is needed for them to regulate. Given the highly stimulating nature of cafeterias with the movement of students, echoing conversations, and amalgam of smells, students can become easily distracted and find it difficult to focus on eating (this is true for students with and without an SPD). Because eating is such a sensory-rich activity, as we explored in Chapter 9, some students may restrict their diets as a result of feeling overstimulated from the tastes, textures, and temperatures, while other students may feel understimulated if there isn't enough variety or intensity of tastes, textures, or temperatures.[5] Oftentimes students with limited diets will eat the same type of food, or food from a particular package or brand, because it is familiar and safe. For these students it is important not to pressure them to try new foods, use incentives to eat more, or hide non-preferred food in a preferred food; all of these compromise your relationship with that student and can actually lead to traumatic experiences.

We know from research that children who eat increased amounts of omega-3 fatty acids—contained in foods like avocado, fish, almonds, and yogurt—perform better in school and have fewer school-related behavioral concerns.[6] Protein-rich foods like beans, eggs, chicken, nuts, and cheese, are also integral for learning. This is because fat and protein are essential for the development of white matter in a child's brain—the axonal connections that integrate different areas of the brain necessary for learning. Protein and omega-3 fatty acids are also essential for clear thinking and concentration. Therefore, what caregivers pack in their child's lunch can certainly influence the learning process.

As adults, what we eat throughout the day also matters. Eating whole-grains, fruits and vegetables, and smaller portions can positively influence the gut. When possible, choose foods that are nutrient-dense rather than processed or additive-filled foods, limit your consumption of high-sugar and high-fat foods, and try to eat non-genetically modified organic foods. All of these can improve what is being communicated between the gut and brain, which can positively influence your state of regulation and physiological state.[7] While food certainly impacts our emotional state, our emotional state can actually impact what is happening in the gut. Stress and anxiety, for example, can influence the digestive system, resulting in conditions such as irritable bowel syndrome, chronic constipation, indigestion, and heartburn.[7] This reinforces the need for you to take the time for self-care, as challenging as that may seem with all the responsibilities you juggle as a teacher (and caregiver). Spend ten minutes each morning and evening doing yoga or a mindfulness activity, grab coffee with or call a supportive friend twice a week, read 20 pages per night of an engaging book, or take a short walk each day at lunch.

School is the perfect environment to talk with students about all of these factors. How do students feel when they are hungry and trying to learn versus when they are satiated and trying to learn? How do students feel when they enter the cafeteria to eat? What are some perceived sensory barriers for students when it comes to snack and lunch time? What ideas do students have for integrating healthier foods into their diet? What are some fat- and protein-rich foods that students already eat? What are some fat- and protein-rich foods that students would like to try? All of these questions can raise awareness for both the students and teacher, as well as empower students to reflect on their diet. Plus, this gives teachers the opportunity to differentiate a fat versus a protein or a fruit versus a vegetable, examine the impact of food on our brain and body, and highlight different signals the body gives us to identify hunger and thirst.

Given all this information, here are some basic things that we recommend to help boost the quantity and quality of food students eat at school in order to facilitate appropriate regulation:

- Teachers can have fat- and protein-rich foods on-hand in the classroom in case a student needs a little "boost" during the day

- Teachers can take snack breaks within the classroom if they find that the scheduled snack breaks are not enough

- Teachers can allow students to have water bottles at their desk to ensure proper water intake

- Teachers can encourage caregivers to send food in packages and containers that the student can open easily

- Teachers can encourage caregivers to send food in see-through containers so the student can readily see what food they have

- Teachers can send home a list of fat- and protein-rich foods to encourage caregivers to pack at least two items in their lunch/snack box

- Teachers can advocate for longer lunch periods to allow students more time to eat

- Teachers can advocate for healthier school lunch options for students

Influence of Screen Time

Screen time can be helpful for children to slow down, veg out, and relax after a busy day—or while caregivers need to make dinner, do chores, or respond to emails. It can also be helpful in the classroom to reinforce what the teacher has taught, provide a multi-media experience, or let the student explore the world of technology. What many people don't realize is that screen time provides a large amount of visual and auditory stimulation while at the same time depriving the body of tactile, proprioceptive, and vestibular input. This imbalance of sensory input can be quite dysregulating for many children. When children come off of screens they can appear like they have an SPD because their brain is craving movement and touch experiences.

Adult brains are also influenced by screen time. Studies indicate higher levels of depression and obesity among adults who spend considerable amounts of time on a screen.[8,9] Even adult brains continue to change, albeit slower than children's, due to neuroplasticity. Screen time can thus interfere with executive functioning skills (such as planning, organizing, working memory, and self-control), creativity and self-reflection, and sustained attention. Too much screen time interferes with the ability not only to connect to others—like your students—but also to connect with yourself.

It is also important to consider what screen time is replacing. There are only a certain number of hours in a day; so if a 9-year-old child is on the screen *outside of school* for an average of four hours, as indicated by research from Common Sense Media, that means four hours less of face-to-face interactions with peers, or time exploring outside, or engaging with hands-on manipulatives and toys.[10] This is true within the school environment as well. It is important that you consider not only how engagement with technology can enhance a student's learning experience but also what activity the technology is replacing. Students learn best with interactive, hands-on, multisensory activities. We operate in a 3-D world and the 2-D screen-based experience can impede the learning process—particularly with regards to one's body and spatial awareness. In fact, research supports that handwriting yields increased test scores, improved integration of concepts, and improved recall of information for students compared to typing.[11,12]

As adults we may not consider the things which screen time replaces. It may even seem like a form of self-care; relaxing with a device to take your mind off of other stressors. Yet this is actually more like brain candy—empty calories of self-care. Consider that 20 minutes checking social media or playing a game could be time spent engaging in more regulating, brain-healthy self-care: reading a book, talking with a colleague, meditating, or doing yoga. We're not suggesting that you cut out screen time altogether, just that you reflect on how your investment in screens is impacting your investment in other things.

Some children, particularly those with an SPD, may use screen time as their primary (or only) way to help regulate or calm their body down. This can be problematic because children need to learn other ways to help regulate themselves and pay attention to cues from their bodies. Children also need to be able to co-regulate with safe, trusting adults and peers as a means to facilitate self-regulation. It is therefore important for both caregivers and teachers to find other ways in which a student with SPD can calm their body. Refer back to Chapters 4–9 as a starting place for regulating activities.

Additionally, screen time systematically provides children with dopamine "hits" in order to reinforce the desire to engage with the device.[3] Dopamine is a powerful neurotransmitter that plays an important role in feelings of pleasure, attention, impulse control, and learning. Too much dopamine release, however, can have negative implications for learning and engagement. Sustained attention may be impacted because students are expecting a reward every couple of minutes (or seconds!) like they receive on a screen. Research suggests that passive screen time (watching a show or video) may actually be better than active screen time (playing an educational game) because there is less frequent release of dopamine.[3] Screen time can also negatively impact the white matter connections within the brain, which are crucial for the integration of different areas of the brain.[12] Replacing screen time with multisensory learning, curious exploration of the world, interactive board games and puzzles, and outdoor play can facilitate white matter connectivity for a more integrated brain.

The American Association of Pediatrics (AAP) recommends that for children 2–5 years old screen time be limited to one hour per day of "high quality programming," such as educational shows.[14] Splitting up screen time into 20-minute increments is best for most children in order to mitigate the imbalance of sensory stimulation. However, some children can tolerate 30 minutes without negative implications while others can only tolerate 10 minutes—this is where caregivers' observations can be particularly helpful. Sitting with a child when watching a show can help engage them in conversations later about what happened and how to apply the concepts during play and social interactions.[9] Teachers should also be asking questions and stimulating conversations about what students have engaged with during screen time at school.

So what does this mean for you, as teachers? Consider the following action-steps:

- Limit screen time in your classroom to two hours per day
- Split up screen time into smaller chunks—less than 20 minutes at a time
- Engage students in conversations and activities that help them integrate the information they learned when on the screen
- Consider using more passive screen activities rather than active screen activities
- Engage students in conversations about the positives and negatives of screen time
- Encourage students to develop a personal plan for screen time (what they will do on the screen, how long they will be on the screen, when they will be on the screen, what they can do when they're not on the screen), both within the school environment and at home
- Encourage students to talk about what they're engaging with on the screen, particularly outside of school

Here are some ways that you, as a teacher, can limit your screen time use during the course of a day in order to be more regulated and engaged with your students:

- Designate screen-free zones in your classroom and home (e.g., student desk area, bedroom)
- Designate screen-free times in your classroom and home (e.g., when eating, the first hour you wake up, one to two hours before bed)
- Turn off your phone during classroom instruction
- Set an alarm for 20 minutes when accessing social media or emails to signify that you need to stand up to take a break
- Delete gaming or social media apps that you find consume a large chunk of your day
- Ask that family and friends wait until after the school day to text or call, unless it is an emergency

As you can see, sleep, diet, and screen time can have a considerable impact on the regulation of a student, as well as your regulation as a teacher. These three factors can cause us to be more sensitive to sensory input, result in increased use of sensory input as a means of regulation, or even mimic the symptoms of SPD. By asking questions about sleep, diet, and screen time use, you can discern why a student may be behaving in a certain way, or discover why you may be more dysregulated on a given day. If you suspect that lack of sleep, inadequate diet, or increased use of screen time may be impacting a student's ability to participate in school-related activities then consider speaking with the caregivers, bearing in mind cultural differences and social justice factors, using the strategies outlined above.

References

1. Paruthi, S., Brooks, L. J., D'Ambrosio, C., Hall, W. A., Kotagal, S., Lloyd, R. M., & Rosen, C. L. (2016). Recommended amount of sleep for pediatric populations: A consensus statement of the American Academy of Sleep Medicine. *Journal of Clinical Sleep Medicine, 12*(6), 785–786.

2. Vasak, M., Williamson, J., Garden, J., & Zwicker, J. G. (2015). Sensory processing and sleep in typically developing infants and toddlers. *American Journal of Occupational Therapy, 69*(4), 6904220040p1– 6904220040p8.

3. Kardaras, N. (2016). *Glow Kids: How Screen Addiction Is Hijacking Our Kids—and How to Break the Trance.* London: St Martin's Press.

4. Consensus Conference Panel, Watson, N. F., Badr, M. S., Belenky, G., Bliwise, D. L., Buxton, O. M., & Kushida, C. (2015). Recommended amount of sleep for a healthy adult: A joint consensus statement of the American Academy of Sleep Medicine and Sleep Research Society. *Journal of Clinical Sleep Medicine, 11*(6), 591–592.

5. Farrow, C. V., & Coulthard, H. (2012). Relationships between sensory sensitivity, anxiety and selective eating in children. *Appetite, 58*(3), 842–846.

6. Gómez-Pinilla, F. (2008). Brain foods: The effects of nutrients on brain function. *Nature Reviews Neuroscience, 9*(7): 568 DOI: 10.1038/nrn2421

7. Mayer, E. (2016). *The Mind-Gut Connection: How the Hidden Conversation within Our Bodies Impacts Our Mood, Our Choices, and Our Overall Health.* New York: Harper Wave.

8. Madhav, K. C., Sherchand, S. P., & Sherchan, S. (2017). Association between screen time and depression among US adults. *Preventive Medicine Reports, 8*, 67–71.

9. Siddarth, D. (2013). Risk factors for obesity in children and adults. *Journal of Investigative Medicine, 61*(6), 1039–1042.

10. American Psychological Association. (2020, April). What do we really know about kids and screens? *Monitor on Psychology, 51*(3). http://www.apa.org/monitor/2020/04/cover-kids-screens

11. Duran, K. S., & Frederick, C. M. (2013). Information comprehension: Handwritten vs. typed notes. *Undergraduate Research Journal for the Human Sciences, 12*(1).

12. Smoker, T. J., Murphy, C. E., & Rockwell, A. K. (2009, October). Comparing memory for handwriting versus typing. *Proceedings of the Human Factors and Ergonomics Society Annual Meeting, 53*(22), 1744–1747.

13. Hutton, J. S., Dudley, J., Horowitz-Kraus, T., DeWitt, T., & Holland, S. K. (2020). Associations between screen-based media use and brain white matter integrity in preschool-aged children. *JAMA pediatrics, 174*(1), e193869–e193869.

14. AAP Council on Communications and Media. (2016). Media and young minds. *Pediatrics, 138*(5), e20162591.

Concluding Thoughts

We hope this book provides you with another lens through which you can see behavior and provide support for students who may present with various challenges in the classroom. As you can see, sensory processing plays a foundational role in the learning process. When the brain is not appropriately responding to and utilizing sensory information, it can interfere with a student's regulation, curiosity, attention, engagement, understanding of self, and meaningful participation. Teachers, you have a powerful role in recognizing, responding to, changing the environment, and seeking additional support for students who experience sensory processing differences. You now have the tools to reflect on your own sensory preferences, as well as your sleep patterns, diet, and screen time habits, in order to better influence your state of regulation. This is a necessary first step in helping to co-regulate with students, especially those with sensory processing needs who may be experiencing difficulty at school.

Both the authors, Jamie and Ashley, have found the information regarding sensory processing to be transformative in their professional and personal lives. Not only has it changed the way in which we work with students, but it has also impacted us personally in how we are aware of and able to care for ourselves and our own children. This information helps to bring an awareness and sensitivity to what might be triggering us as well as how to support ourselves into getting back into a regulated state. One of the authors, Ashley, is very sensitive to noise. Crowded, noisy environments are very overwhelming for her. She notices that she becomes very exhausted quickly when she is in a crowded or noisy environment.

Knowing this helps her plan ahead so that she can support herself and her own regulation when going into a situation such as this. The other author, Jamie, finds running to be a very regulating vestibular-based sensory experience. She makes sure to carve out time each morning to run as a form of self-care to increase her ability to co-regulate with her children and clients. Knowing what sensory input is regulating or dysregulating for you as a teacher, as well as for the students and children in your life, can improve not only the quality of your life but the lives of those around you.

We know that there is a lot of information in this book that may feel complex and unfamiliar. Just like anything new, it may feel overwhelming or difficult to implement. Luckily, from what we know about the brain and neuroplasticity, the more we use it the easier it will get! We suggest starting with one or two sensory-smart strategies and building up from there. If anything, a new awareness about sensory processing can give you foundational knowledge about what may be underlying the behaviors you see in your students, ultimately giving you a starting point to ask new or different questions.

Instead of moving the behavior clothespin down the chart because a student is not sitting still, first wonder about that student's processing of vestibular input. Instead of reprimanding a student for covering their ears and screaming in a loud auditorium, first explore how they are processing auditory information. Instead of keeping a student inside from recess for not completing their work, consider first how the sensory input from recess will actually help them regulate in order to better attend to seated activities. Instead of assuming a student is being manipulative or defiant, be curious about their processing of interoceptive input that results in them needing to use the bathroom frequently. Instead of hanging various student projects on the walls and from the ceiling, notice first how too much visual input impacts your level of stress and attention. You can then look to this book to find many sensory-smart strategies to support yourself and your students. You can also serve as a protective relationship for a student with an SPD to buffer the toxic stress they feel at school. And remember that you can also always reach out to your school's occupational therapist for additional support.

Maintaining an open, curious, and reflective stance with ourselves and with the students we work with can support not only our success, but also lead to the most positive outcomes for our students. Start small, and keep sensory processing in mind when managing behaviors in your classroom. We appreciate you and the work you do daily to support students. Don't forget to support your needs as well so that you can remain more regulated and serve as a protective, co-regulating relationship for your students.

Appendix A
Movement Activities
for the Classroom

Note: These are taken from Chaves, J., & Taylor, A. (2020). *The "Why" Behind Classroom Behaviors: Integrative Strategies for Learning, Regulation, and Relationships*. Thousand Oaks, CA: Corwin.

Use this list of activities to celebrate movement in the classroom while promoting sensory integration. *Active-Play, Active-Learning (APAL), a program funded by the Michael & Susan Dell Center for Healthy Living, also has physically active, fun strategies for movement breaks that can be integrated into various aspects of learning.*

When are good times for movement?

- At the beginning of the day
- Before starting a new activity
- After a long period (>20–30 minutes) of seated learning
- Before transitioning to a new classroom or new subject
- While waiting in line
- When you notice your students need a break

What are good movement activities?
Short duration (<2 minutes)

- Chair push-ups
- Wall push-ups
- Jumping jacks
- Windmills

- Stretches—hands, fingers, arms, legs, back, neck
- "Head-Shoulder-Knees-and-Toes" song
- Deep breathing while placing your hand on different body parts
- Body squeezes
- "Tense and Release"

Medium duration (2–5 minutes)

- Yoga
- "Shake Your Sillies Out"
- "GoNoodle" songs
- Dance break
- Freeze dance
- Pass a ball around the class (while standing at their chairs or in a circle)
- March around the class
- "Simon Says"

Long duration (>5 minutes)

- Yoga
- Make a "rain storm" (using your hands and feet)
- "Pass the beat" (e.g., clap, clap, stomp, stomp) around the class
- Human knot challenge
- Classroom scavenger hunt

In addition to these more structured activities, set up guidelines for other student-led, movement-based options in the classroom. This can not only empower the students, but also give them more independence and bolster your trust in them.

- Let students sit where they choose for silent reading
- Allow students to make choices about flexible seating
- Assign student responsibilities each day: taking attendance, passing out papers, collecting papers, getting out classroom-based journals

or notebooks, picking up scraps, setting the activity timer, and erasing the board

- Give students the option to stand if needed after a certain period of time (e.g., 20 minutes)
- Provide a bin of appropriate fidgets that students can access

Appendix B
Multisensory
Learning Activities

Note: These are taken from Chaves, J., & Taylor, A. (2020). *The "Why" Behind Classroom Behaviors: Integrative Strategies for Learning, Regulation, and Relationships.* Thousand Oaks, CA: Corwin.

Use this list of multisensory learning activities to help promote sensory integration and overall brain integration.

Math

- Play hopscotch when adding, subtracting, multiplying, or dividing numbers and have students record their answers on a sheet of paper
- Roll dice to do multiplication tables, squares, greater than/less than, adding numbers, subtracting numbers
- Use dominoes to do greater than/less than, adding numbers, subtracting numbers, multiplying numbers, and dividing numbers
- In pairs, roll a ball back and forth or use a zoom ball to complete multiplication tables
- Use fun tactile manipulatives as counters, such as mini porcupine balls, cotton balls, pasta shapes, or stickers
- Use dot art markers for counting, adding, subtracting, multiplying, or dividing
- Create "math facts" songs or poems—you can do this individually as a teacher, in small groups, or as a whole classroom
- Do math facts while playing clapping games

- Put math flashcards in a bin of rice, sand, beans, or dried pasta, and then have each student draw out a flashcard and give the answer (you can do this as a whole classroom or in small groups with different tactile bins and have students rotate)
- Trace math facts "in the air" with your finger
- In small groups, have students complete math facts with their bodies (e.g., one student makes his body into the number 1, one student makes her body into a plus sign, one student makes her body into the number 2, one student makes his body into an equal sign, and one student makes his body into the number 3)
- Explore the classroom to find different shapes and/or examples of symmetry
- Play math bowling: put a number of the bottom of each bowling pin and have students roll a ball to knock down the pins. The small group can work together to solve the math problem (e.g., add all the numbers, subtract all the numbers).

Reading

- Listen to an audiobook while following along in a written book
- Have the student stand up when reading aloud
- Have the student hold something tactile (stuffed animal, stress ball, fidget toy) when it is his turn to read
- Sit or stand in different places in the room during silent reading
- Play classical music in the background during silent reading
- Stomp, clap, or tap along to word syllables
- Pair each sight word with a movement
- Play reading bowling: put a sight word or vocabulary word on the bottom of each bowling pin and have students roll a ball to knock down the pins. The small group can work together to read the words and/or define the words.

Spelling and Writing

- Sit or stand in different places in the room
- Draw a picture to go along with what you wrote

- Use thought bubbles, idea charts, and graphic organizers
- Break up into groups and act out journal responses, essay outlines, and narrative ideas
- Use different pencil colors for different drafts of writings or different writing assignments
- Use individual dry erase boards with dry erase crayons (or individual chalkboards with chalk)
- Trace letters or spell out words "in the air" using a finger
- Do "yoga writing" by making different letters with your body
- Do spelling activities with magnetic letters
- Find and cut out spelling words from magazines—then glue them onto paper to make them into a sentence
- In pairs, roll a ball back and forth or use a zoom ball to spell out different words

Note: The Learning Without Tears curriculum has a variety of multisensory activities that can be integrated into writing and spelling activities.

Social Studies and History

- Create maps and map keys using different craft materials, such as yarn, tissue paper, glitter (every teacher's favorite!), sequins, pom poms, etc.
- Bring in compasses and have groups of students follow a set of compass directions to reach an end goal/prize
- Encourage students to reference a globe when talking about geography
- Show pictures and play sounds from different geographic regions
- Have each student cut out an individual state and work as a class to create a map of the United States
- Use "dress up" as a way to have students emulate famous people in history
- Act out important stories in history after reading about them
- Put important dates or events on flashcards and have students place them in order or match them up

Appendix C
Sensory Preference
Checklist

Use this checklist to determine your sensory preferences, as well as the sensory preferences of students in your classroom. Better understanding sensory preferences can help you structure your classroom's sensory environment and respect the sensory needs of students.

Note: This checklist was adapted from the TherapyWorks "How Does Your Engine Run?" program (Williams, M. S., & Shellenberger, S., 1996).

	Improve Regulation/ Attention	Disrupt Regulation/ Attention	Neutral
Tactile			
Twist your hair	☐	☐	☐
Fidget with a toy	☐	☐	☐
Move something around in your pocket with your hand	☐	☐	☐
Bend a straw	☐	☐	☐
Pick at your cuticle or nails	☐	☐	☐
Pet a dog or cat	☐	☐	☐
Drum fingers or pencil on table	☐	☐	☐
Rub your fingers on your lips	☐	☐	☐
Rub feet together	☐	☐	☐
Twist a sweatshirt string around your finger	☐	☐	☐

	Improve Regulation/ Attention	Disrupt Regulation/ Attention	Neutral
Visual			
Look out an open window	☐	☐	☐
Turn off the lights	☐	☐	☐
Open the blinds/drapes	☐	☐	☐
Go outside in the sun	☐	☐	☐
Wear sunglasses	☐	☐	☐
Watch a fish swim in a tank	☐	☐	☐
Watch a fast-paced TV show	☐	☐	☐
Look at something spinning	☐	☐	☐
Move something quickly across your face	☐	☐	☐
People moving around you	☐	☐	☐
Sit in the front of the class	☐	☐	☐
Sit in the back of the class	☐	☐	☐
Auditory			
Listen to classical music	☐	☐	☐
Hear a scratch on a chalkboard	☐	☐	☐
Listen to hard rock	☐	☐	☐
Work with other people talking	☐	☐	☐
Listen to others hum or sing	☐	☐	☐
Hear a fire siren or fire alarm	☐	☐	☐
Work in a coffee shop	☐	☐	☐
Work in quiet room	☐	☐	☐
Sing or talk to self	☐	☐	☐
Hear a dog barking (almost constantly)	☐	☐	☐

	Improve Regulation/ Attention	Disrupt Regulation/ Attention	Neutral
Hear the toilet flushing or hand dryer	☐	☐	☐
Hear a clock ticking	☐	☐	☐
Hear an air conditioner buzzing	☐	☐	☐
Movement			
Rock your body slightly when sitting	☐	☐	☐
Bounce your legs	☐	☐	☐
Sit upside-down on a chair or couch	☐	☐	☐
Swing back and forth	☐	☐	☐
Stand while working or eating	☐	☐	☐
Sit or bounce on a yoga ball	☐	☐	☐
Doodle while listening	☐	☐	☐
Kick your legs back and forth while sitting	☐	☐	☐
Push a chair back on two legs while sitting	☐	☐	☐
Walk around while talking	☐	☐	☐
Pace back and forth while thinking	☐	☐	☐
Tap pencil or pen	☐	☐	☐
Go for a run or walk	☐	☐	☐
Oral/Taste			
Drink everything through a straw	☐	☐	☐
Chew gum	☐	☐	☐
Eat popcorn or trail mix	☐	☐	☐
Suck on hard candy	☐	☐	☐
Crunch on nuts, pretzels or chips	☐	☐	☐

	Improve Regulation/ Attention	Disrupt Regulation/ Attention	Neutral
Crunch or suck on ice pieces	☐	☐	☐
Eat hot soup	☐	☐	☐
"Chew" on pencil/pen	☐	☐	☐
Eat mints or cinnamon candies	☐	☐	☐
Chew on straws	☐	☐	☐
Chew on shirt sleeves or shirt collar	☐	☐	☐
Bite on nails or cuticles	☐	☐	☐
Drink carbonated drink	☐	☐	☐
Chew on sweatshirt strings	☐	☐	☐
Whistle while you work	☐	☐	☐
Make popping noises with your lips	☐	☐	☐
Suck, lick, bite on your lips or the inside of your cheeks	☐	☐	☐
Smell			
Smell markers	☐	☐	☐
Smell perfume, cologne, or scented lotion	☐	☐	☐
Smell body odor or feet	☐	☐	☐
Smell flowers	☐	☐	☐
Smell trash or fertilizer	☐	☐	☐

Appendix D
Flexible Seating
Options

Ball Chair
- Switches between sitting and standing
- Switches position in chair
- Needs extra vestibular input
- Sensitive to hard texture of seat

Wobble Stool
- Switches position in chair
- Rock back and forth on chair legs
- Needs extra vestibular input

T-Stool
- Switches position in chair
- Needs extra vestibular input
- Difficulty sitting upright
- Needs extra proprioceptive input

Core Disc
- Switches position in chair
- Sensitive to hard texture of seat
- Difficulty sitting upright

TheraBand on Front of Chair
- Switches position in chair
- Difficulty sitting upright
- Needs extra proprioceptive input

Bean Bag Chairs (not recommended for writing activities)
- Difficulty sitting upright
- Sensitive to hard texture of seat
- Sits too close to peers
- Needs a calming space

Scoop Rockers (not recommended for writing activities)
- Difficulty sitting upright
- Sits too close to peers
- Needs extra vestibular input

Appendix E
Classroom Quick-
Reference Sheets

Use these quick-reference sheets as reminders for ways you can recognize and support the sensory differences of certain students, as well as ways you can build a sensory-smart classroom for all your students.

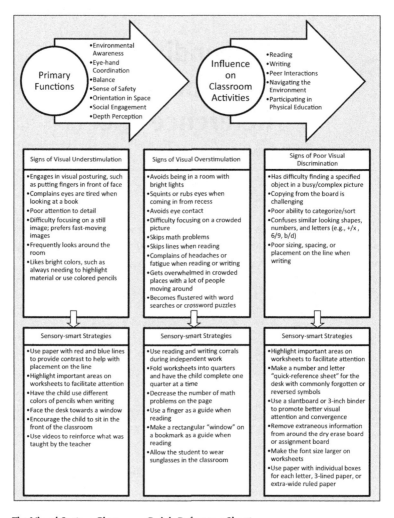

The Visual System Classroom Quick-Reference Sheet

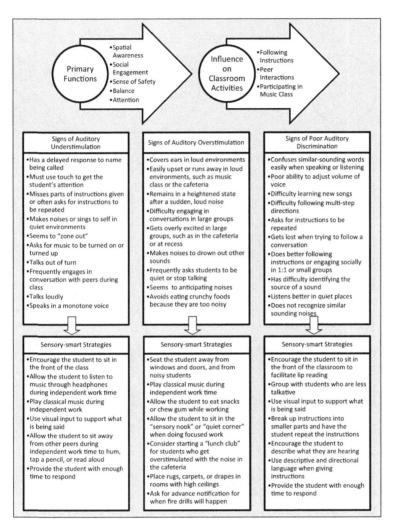

Primary Functions
•Spatial Awareness
•Social Engagement
•Sense of Safety
•Balance
•Attention

Influence on Classroom Activities
•Following Instructions
•Peer Interactions
•Participating in Music Class

Signs of Auditory Understimulation	Signs of Auditory Overstimulation	Signs of Poor Auditory Discrimination
•Has a delayed response to name being called •Must use touch to get the student's attention •Misses parts of instructions given or often asks for instructions to be repeated •Makes noises or sings to self in quiet environments •Seems to "zone out" •Asks for music to be turned on or turned up •Talks out of turn •Frequently engages in conversation with peers during class •Talks loudly •Speaks in a monotone voice	•Covers ears in loud environments •Easily upset or runs away in loud environments, such as music class or the cafeteria •Remains in a heightened state after a sudden, loud noise •Difficulty engaging in conversations in large groups •Gets overly excited in large groups, such as in the cafeteria or at recess •Makes noises to drown out other sounds •Frequently asks students to be quiet or stop talking •Seems to anticipating noises •Avoids eating crunchy foods because they are too noisy	•Confuses similar-sounding words easily when speaking or listening •Poor ability to adjust volume of voice •Difficulty learning new songs •Difficulty following multi-step directions •Asks for instructions to be repeated •Gets lost when trying to follow a conversation •Does better following instructions or engaging socially in 1:1 or small groups •Has difficulty identifying the source of a sound •Listens better in quiet places •Does not recognize similar sounding noises
Sensory-smart Strategies	**Sensory-smart Strategies**	**Sensory-smart Strategies**
•Encourage the student to sit in the front of the class •Allow the student to listen to music through headphones during independent work time •Play classical music during independent work •Use visual input to support what is being said •Allow the student to sit away from other peers during independent work time to hum, tap a pencil, or read aloud •Provide the student with enough time to respond	•Seat the student away from windows and doors, and from noisy students •Play classical music during independent work time •Allow the student to eat snacks or chew gum while working •Allow the student to sit in the "sensory nook" or "quiet corner" when doing focused work •Consider starting a "lunch club" for students who get overstimulated with the noise in the cafeteria •Place rugs, carpets, or drapes in rooms with high ceilings •Ask for advance notification for when fire drills will happen	•Encourage the student to sit in the front of the classroom to facilitate lip reading •Group with students who are less talkative •Use visual input to support what is being said •Break up instructions into smaller parts and have the student repeat the instructions •Encourage the student to describe what they are hearing •Use descriptive and directional language when giving instructions •Provide the student with enough time to respond

The Auditory System Classroom Quick-Reference Sheet

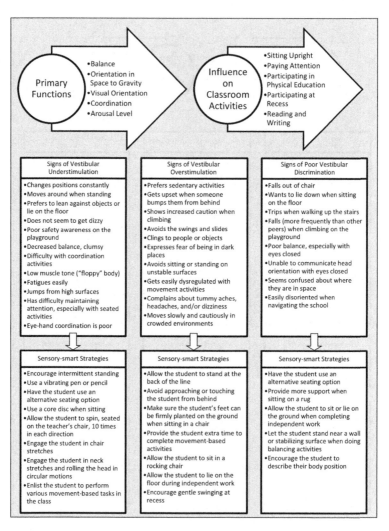

The Vestibular System Classroom Quick-Reference Sheet

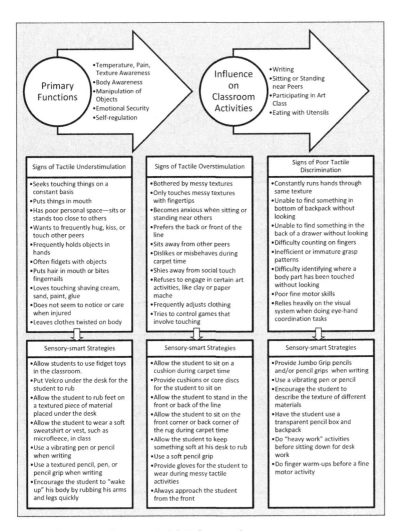

The Tactile System Classroom Quick-Reference Sheet

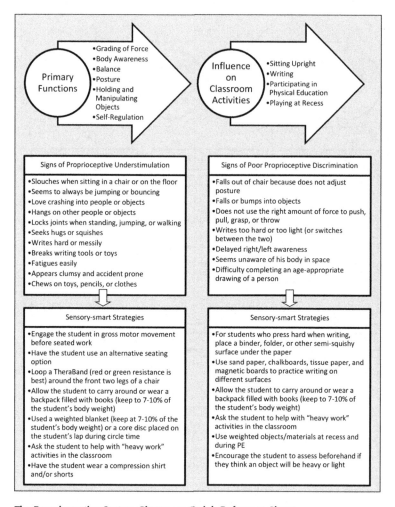

The Proprioceptive System Classroom Quick-Reference Sheet

Note: Typically overstimulation to proprioceptive input is not seen in children; it is more likely a sign that the vestibular system or tactile system is overstimulated. This is because the proprioceptive system provides primarily inhibitory information to the brain, not excitatory information.

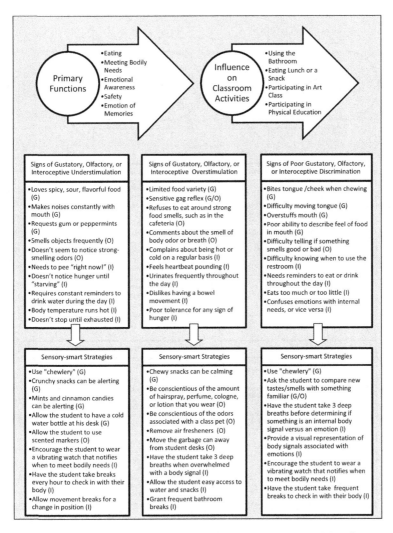

Primary Functions
- Eating
- Meeting Bodily Needs
- Emotional Awareness
- Safety
- Emotion of Memories

Influence on Classroom Activities
- Using the Bathroom
- Eating Lunch or a Snack
- Participating in Art Class
- Participating in Physical Education

Signs of Gustatory, Olfactory, or Interoceptive Understimulation	Signs of Gustatory, Olfactory, or Interoceptive Overstimulation	Signs of Poor Gustatory, Olfactory, or Interoceptive Discrimination
• Loves spicy, sour, flavorful food (G) • Makes noises constantly with mouth (G) • Requests gum or peppermints (G) • Smells objects frequently (O) • Doesn't seem to notice strong-smelling odors (O) • Needs to pee "right now!" (I) • Doesn't notice hunger until "starving" (I) • Requires constant reminders to drink water during the day (I) • Body temperature runs hot (I) • Doesn't stop until exhausted (I)	• Limited food variety (G) • Sensitive gag reflex (G/O) • Refuses to eat around strong food smells, such as in the cafeteria (O) • Comments about the smell of body odor or breath (O) • Complains about being hot or cold on a regular basis (I) • Feels heartbeat pounding (I) • Urinates frequently throughout the day (I) • Dislikes having a bowel movement (I) • Poor tolerance for any sign of hunger (I)	• Bites tongue /cheek when chewing (G) • Difficulty moving tongue (G) • Overstuffs mouth (G) • Poor ability to describe feel of food in mouth (G) • Difficulty telling if something smells good or bad (O) • Difficulty knowing when to use the restroom (I) • Needs reminders to eat or drink throughout the day (I) • Eats too much or too little (I) • Confuses emotions with internal needs, or vice versa (I)

Sensory-smart Strategies	Sensory-smart Strategies	Sensory-smart Strategies
• Use "chewlery" (G) • Crunchy snacks can be alerting (G) • Mints and cinnamon candies can be alerting (G) • Allow the student to have a cold water bottle at his desk (G) • Allow the student to use scented markers (O) • Encourage the student to wear a vibrating watch that notifies when to meet bodily needs (I) • Have the student take breaks every hour to check in with their body (I) • Allow movement breaks for a change in position (I)	• Chewy snacks can be calming (G) • Be conscientious of the amount of hairspray, perfume, cologne, or lotion that you wear (O) • Be conscientious of the odors associated with a class pet (O) • Remove air fresheners (O) • Move the garbage can away from student desks (O) • Have the student take 3 deep breaths when overwhelmed with a body signal (I) • Allow the student easy access to water and snacks (I) • Grant frequent bathroom breaks (I)	• Use "chewlery" (G) • Ask the student to compare new tastes/smells with something familiar (G/O) • Have the student take 3 deep breaths before determining if something is an internal body signal versus an emotion (I) • Provide a visual representation of body signals associated with emotions (I) • Encourage the student to wear a vibrating watch that notifies when to meet bodily needs (I) • Have the student take frequent breaks to check in with their body (I)

The Gustatory, Olfactory, and Interoceptive Systems Classroom Quick-Reference Sheet

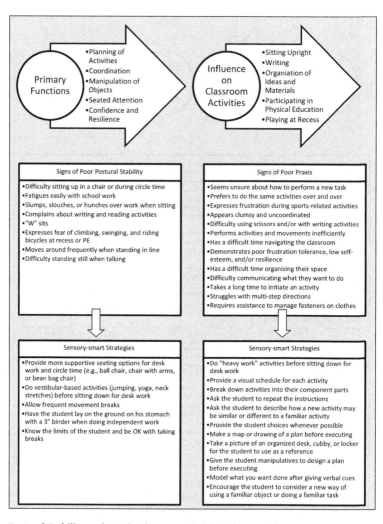

Postural Stability and Praxis Classroom Quick-Reference Sheet

Made in the USA
Coppell, TX
09 June 2021